How to Sell a House When It's Worth Less Than the Mortgage

Options for "Underwater" Homeowners and Investors

Dwan Bent-Twyford
Bill Twyford

WILEY

John Wiley & Sons, Inc.

For general information on our other products and services or for technical support,
please contact our Customer Care Department within the United States at
(800) 762-2974, outside the United States at (317) 572-3993 or fax (317) 572-4002.

Wiley also publishes its books in a variety of electronic formats. Some content that
appears in print may not be available in electronic books. For more information about
Wiley products, visit our web site at www.wiley.com.

ISBN 978-0-470-41861-1

Printed in the United States of America.

10 9 8 7 6 5 4 3 2 1

CONTENTS

PART III
OTHER OPTIONS AND ISSUES FOR UNDERWATER HOMEOWNERS

If you have any problems downloading these forms, please contact our office at (303) 838-5532.

How Did So Many of Us End Up with Underwater Houses

If you are like many homeowners today, you feel overwhelmed by what is supposed to be the American dream—homeownership. We have this vision of what it is supposed to be like—cute house, white picket fence, a couple of kids, a dog in the backyard, summer barbecues, family time, and so much more.

We find a house and fall in love with it. We then find a mortgage broker who offers us an amazing deal—zero down or a low down payment or low fixed payments for two years or something along those lines. We buy the house, move in, and all is right with the world.

Soon, our two-year low monthly payment resets, the payment rises, then it resets again and the payment continues to rise. Now the stress of making our mortgage payment is all we think about and we become disillusioned with our American dream.

The dream continues to crumble when you try to sell your house to get free of the payments only to find that property values have dropped nationwide and you now owe more than your house is worth. Sadly, there are hundreds of thousands of houses on the market that aren't selling because folks, just like you, owe more than their house is worth.

If you have the time and money, you can wait out the market and sell your property when values come back up. If you are like most Americans, you don't have the time or resources to wait it out. You want to be relieved of the stress today.

Many of you reading this book might be another type of homeowner—**real estate investors disillusioned by the**

dream of getting rich buying and selling real estate. There are so many late-night television shows that make real estate investing seem like a breeze. You bought a property hoping to make some money on it, and now it's costing you more than you can afford—every month.

The good news is that there are many solutions available that most people don't know exist. **Did you know that you can negotiate with your bank to accept less than you currently owe as full payment?** Are you aware that there are government programs that will allow you to rent out your house for three times the current market rents? No matter where you are in your property situation—there is a solution for you.

Education is power. As you read this book, you will begin to realize that you are not alone *and* that there are solutions to your problem. You will be able to sleep again, you will have less stress in your life, and the best part is—you can start fresh and own another home again and continue the American dream—homeownership ***with knowledge!***

As we write this, there are almost two million people in foreclosure with the numbers expected to rise. What is a nation to do when foreclosures are on the rise? We must band together to help as many people as possible. Our company has completed over 1,800 personal transactions and coached thousands more through tough situations to help homeowners walk away from homes they could no longer afford.

Our goal is to educate you on several different options—that you can do yourself—and to help you pick the option that best suits your needs. There is no reason for you to lie awake at night worrying about what you will do, or how you will make your mortgage payment or when the market will change or anything else that is negative and sucks the life out of you.

What Happened to Real Estate Prices?

Before we jump into the book, we want to talk about what is currently happening in our economy. In the late 1990s and in the early part of the 2000s, banks used tougher guidelines when homeowners wanted to purchase a property with conventional financing. Banks would lend you money based on your debt-to-income ratio *and* your credit score. Back then, a **maximum** of 30 percent (sometimes up to 40 percent) of your income could be used toward a mortgage payment. For example, if your monthly income was $2,000, you could qualify for a mortgage payment of $600 including principal, interest, taxes, and insurance (PITI). Most investment properties required a 20 percent down payment and proof that you could afford the investment mortgage payment in addition to your residential mortgage payment.

In some cases, the banks would stretch the loan amount allowing 40 percent of your income to be applied toward the mortgage payment.

However, what if you had a car repair, medical bills, needed a home repair, needed to buy clothes, or anything else? Where did the money come from? What about trying to save for retirement or trying to care for ailing parents?

Sometimes life just takes over, you have a problem, you use some of the money that should be used for the mortgage payment, and next thing you know—you are one payment late, then two, then three, then the bank files foreclosure papers, and then everything spirals out of control.

Many investors bought rental properties when they had no landlord experience. When their rentals sat empty, they used their mortgage money to keep up with the rental payments or worse yet, they spent the rental income for their own bills and fell behind on investment properties, which often ended up in foreclosure without the tenants being aware of anything until they were served with eviction papers from the sheriff. Often tenants had to move out in three days. It would stun you to see how many investors are going under right now—you are not alone.

The reason our country is in such a mess is because of the banks trying to boost the economy. Easy loans caused a financial disaster. As we are writing this book, the government just agreed to a "bailout." What does this bailout mean to people facing foreclosure? . . . Nothing. The bailout is going to bail out banks—not distressed homeowners. Folks, this book *IS* the bailout option for you. We are going to show you how to fight the red tape and get a fresh start. Whether you are a homeowner or an investor, you do have options—many options, and we will empower you so that you don't have to worry about a recession or a depression or anything else of that nature. All you have to do is worry about what to do with your new financial status.

Did you know that Henry Ford went bankrupt *five times?* Think about it:

1. He started a company and went bankrupt.
2. He started another company and went bankrupt.
3. He started another company and went bankrupt again.
4. He started yet another company and went bankrupt again.
5. In spite of all the naysayers in his life, he started another company and went bankrupt again.

Then he started Ford Motor Company—who you may be making payments to right now.

If you are an investor losing your investment properties—it's okay. Our advice for the future is not to buy any rentals unless you can afford to make the mortgage payments—in addition to your bills—for five months on all your rentals. For example—say you own five rental properties and the mortgage payment is $500 on each. This means your monthly commitment is $2,500 a month. Unless you can afford to pay $2,500 for five months, in addition to all your regular bills, do not become a landlord, yet. We realize that this seems extreme because it is unlikely that all five of your rentals would be vacant at the same time; however, it does happen. The great news is that in this book we are going to cover some great ways to turn your rentals into cash flow machines again.

The average person's life span is 75 or so. If you are in financial hardship and it takes you three years to recover, in the big picture, it's not that much time. When you recover and start over, you'll have many more good years than bad.

People tend to live above their means in this country. We both like living our spoiled lifestyle; however, we didn't come by it easily. We have both had financial problems in the past, been divorced, suffered foreclosures, and barely gotten by. Through a lot of hard work, cutting back, and many blessings from God, we were able to make it to the top income percentage in the entire country.

Easy Money Home Loans

In the mid-2000s, the mortgage industry came up with what seemed like a good idea—easy loans to boost the economy. These loans were designed to give as many people as possible the chance to live the American dream—property ownership. People are often so focused on owning a home that they are willing to stretch themselves just to do it. This is where it all started to go downhill. Too many people went out on a limb. These creative loans did just what they were supposed to do— boosted the economy. The problem is that no one really thought it *all* the way through.

It also became very easy to buy investment properties. So many people jumped on the bandwagon and invested in more property than they could actually afford. Many investors went to several different banks at the same time and borrowed from more than one just to buy multiple properties. Without landlord experience, owning multiple properties can be a recipe for disaster.

There are several different types of creative loans—still available today—and we're going to spend some time here explaining them to you. See which one your loan falls into, if any.

Interest-Only Loans

These loans were among the most popular. With a typical payment, you pay principle, interest, taxes, and insurance. The bank takes your full monthly payment and uses the money to pay for the various items. The bank keeps the interest and principle portion of the payment and saves the balance to pay the property taxes and the homeowners insurance when they come due.

These loans were extremely popular with investors because they figured property values would continue to climb and they could collect rent for a few years and then sell the properties for a quick profit. Many investors made the smallest payment possible to get as much cash flow as they could. This is called "pick a payment." Unfortunately, it didn't work out very well. Property values fell, the mortgage payments reset to a higher amount, rent didn't cover the new payment, investors' home mortgage payments also reset, gas prices went up, people moved into cheaper rentals, properties became vacant, and investors started losing their shirts across the country.

The biggest problem with interest-only loans is that people borrow based on the payment. If $725 is the most you can afford, you don't buy a house with an interest-only payment of $725. You buy a house with a **PITI** payment of $725. We feel that the lending industry used extremely poor judgment giving loans that people could barely afford with the low interest payment knowing the payment was going to reset soon. Since most of us think in the "here and now," people weren't prepared when their payments started rising.

Like investors, many homeowners figured they would refinance their houses when the new payment came due because property values were rising. Unfortunately, property values dropped and people found themselves owing what their house was worth and they were unable to refinance. The fact that no one could refinance was instrumental in the current recession. Most of the initial interest-only loans were given with a two-, three-, five-, or seven-year fixed rate. This is why foreclosures are going to continue to rise—the three-, five- and seven-year loans haven't reset yet. We have some tough years ahead of us.

Short sales   Negotiating with the bank to accept less than what you owe as payment in full.

If you have one of these loans, don't feel bad. You are not alone. There are millions and millions of people in the same boat. We realize that doesn't make you feel better or solve your problem. We will cover **short sales** soon and you'll begin to see light at the end of the tunnel.

Stated income You don't have to prove to the bank what your income is. You can tell the bank you make $100,000 when you actually make $50,000.

We teach our students to **always** buy a property based on what you can afford today or what it will rent for today—including principle, interest, taxes, and insurance. Don't buy a house based on a possible raise, a new job, low interest payments, or anything other than PITI.

Liar Loans

These loans are killer. They allow a homeowner or an investor to buy a house based on **stated income.** Investors went nuts over these loans. Typically, homeowners as well as investors have to prove their income in order to purchase a property. The more you make, the bigger the house you can afford or the more rentals you can buy. Liar loans allow you to buy a property based on what you "state" that you earn. As long as you had good credit, the banks did not ask for much else. We used to joke that as long as you could fog a mirror, you could get a loan. Unfortunately, you need to do more than fog a mirror to own a home.

You might make $50,000 a year and qualify for a $100,000 property. By stating that you earn $100,000 a year and with an interest-only loan, you could buy a $200,000 property. The problem is that you really only qualify for a $100,000 property based on reality. Again, you have an emergency and next thing you know, you're using your mortgage payment money to pay for things. The term "liar loans" is a bit harsh, but it states exactly what it is—people lied to get a bigger house or to buy more rentals.

It is incredibly important to buy only what you can afford. We know you'd like a bigger house, a bigger yard, a nicer car, and more. We all do. We discovered that when we were both younger (and still didn't know each other) we had a hard time waiting and working for what we wanted. We both bought places we could not afford, ran up too much credit card debt, made bad decisions, went through divorces and foreclosures. Once we met, it seems like God just opened up the world to us and things really started to happen. When we met, we were both doing well financially, but together, we have been unstoppable. There is no shame in making mistakes. What is a shame is **not** to learn from your mistakes and then to continue making them. All of you can make a fresh start, get further ahead, and have more than you have ever dreamed of as long as you learn from the mistakes you made this time around.

If you are in a loan that you can't afford, we'll help you get a fresh start, get into a property you can afford, unload rentals, live stress free, and start again.

HELOC Loans

Homeowners love HELOC loans—**Home Equity Line of Credit**—because you only pay interest on what you borrow. For example—say you originally bought your property for $125,000. Over the years, it has gone up in value—it's now worth $200,000. Instead of refinancing your property for the $200,000 it is now worth, you take a HELOC loan. You get approved for $75,000. Along with the $125,000 on the first mortgage, you also have $75,000 line of credit.

The great thing about a HELOC is that you only pay interest as you use the money. If you use $10,000 of the $75,000 that you are approved for, you only pay interest and payments on the $10,000 you are using. The bad thing is that people often have a hard time controlling a credit line like that. They use the money to pay off credit cards or buy things and then run the credit cards up again and get back into debt. If you used your line of credit to pay credit cards off and then began using them again, now you owe credit cards *and* your credit line is used up.

Many would-be investors use HELOCs to buy rentals. We suggest that you never use your primary residence as collateral to buy investment properties. If things go wrong, you don't want to lose your place of residence.

It is very easy to get into financial trouble with a loan like this. They are easy to get, payments can be low, and it is tempting to buy stuff with the money. You think, "I'll just buy this one thing and then I'll pay it off." Next thing you know, you're buying a second thing and the first one isn't paid off. It doesn't take long to get out of control.

As the debt builds, you decide to refinance your house to pay off the HELOC. The banks are offering an attractive, low monthly, interest-only loan. Property values drop and now you owe more than your house it worth and—boom—you are in financial trouble.

See how easy it is to get into financial trouble? We can't stress enough—only buy what you can afford today! No matter how attractive a loan looks, no matter how low the payments are, no matter what the initial cost to get into the loan ... don't do it unless you can easily afford the principle, interest, taxes, and insurance with the current income you have right this very minute.

When Lending Guidelines Loosened—The Beginning of Our Current Problems

As we mentioned earlier, banks give loans based on your income versus your debt as well as your credit score. If you make $2,000 a month, your mortgage payment would be approximately 30 percent to 40 percent of your income—if you have good credit. This means that your payment could be as high as $800, but no more. The $800 would be principle, interest, taxes, and insurance.

As the 2000s progressed and property values skyrocketed, many banks loosened their lending guidelines to boost the economy. Banks began to allow 50 percent to 60 percent of your income to be used toward a mortgage payment. Most banks offer an 80 percent first mortgage and a 20 percent second mortgage to total what you are borrowing.

For example, if you are borrowing $200,000, you might get $160,000 on a first mortgage and $40,000 on a second mortgage to total $200,000. By borrowing 80 percent on a first mortgage, the banks lessen their risk if you were to default. The riskiest part of a loan is the top 20 percent. If the bank takes the house at the foreclosure sale, it might lose the 20 percent second mortgage, but it would recoup the 80 percent first mortgage by selling the house at the sale or by selling the house later via a real estate agent.

Typically, when you have a first mortgage and a second mortgage, the interest rates are different:

The first mortgage offers lower interest rates, typically has less closing costs, and is a 30-year loan. Based on good credit, you might pay a $6\frac{1}{2}$ percent interest rate and pay two points. A "point" is 1 percent of what you borrow. On a $100,000 house with one point, you would pay $1,000 toward closing costs.

A second mortgage usually has higher interest rates, more closing costs, more points, and is a 10-year loan. You might pay 9 percent interest and have four points at the closing. If the banks give enough second mortgages, they make a lot in points and interest, and it offsets the mortgages they lose in foreclosure.

Let's look at what a 60 percent debt-to-income payment might look like. Say your income is the same $2,000 as in the first section. Instead of a high payment of 40 percent of your income—which is $800—you get an even higher payment that totals 60 percent of your income—which is $1,200. There is an $800 per month first mortgage and a $400 second mortgage. Because the first mortgage is still 40 percent of your income, you qualify for the loan. The second mortgage puts you under each month. Now let's look at the same figures we looked at earlier:

Income	$2,000
Mortgage	$800 first, plus a $400 second
Electric	$150
Car Payment	$300
Gas	$250
Phone	$100
Groceries	$400

You are going in the hole $400 each month. Again, what about savings, emergencies, retirement, kids, ailing parents, and more? People try to juggle things, maybe take a second job, use savings to make mortgage payments, and then they get buried. Things spiral out of control and you lose your house. Along with losing your house, you lose your zest for life, you're embarrassed, you feel like a loser, you think things will never get better, you beat yourself up over where things went wrong, and much more negative energy is wasted. Does this sound like anyone you might know—maybe even you?

Whether you are a homeowner in distress, a real estate investor in distress, or just looking for a great deal for yourself— we have something for you. Please read this book with an open mind. It is never easy to start over, but it may be necessary. We promise, life can be great again. You can own a home, you can invest in rentals, you can become wealthy, you may even share your story and offer encouragement to others . . . we do!

Meet the Authors

Bill and I are like many of you. We wanted to live the American Dream—marriage, children, a home, a white picket fence, a puppy, and so on. Like many of you, we each found ourselves in financial trouble, lost everything, including our houses, and had to start over. All this happened before we even met.

Bill was a painting contractor who was forced to quit painting because it was affecting his lungs. His doctor said that if he wanted to live to be 40, he needed to move to a higher altitude and clean up his lungs. He moved his family from Texas to Colorado and got healthy. He was semiretired for several months and soon began climbing the walls. He decided to go back to work. Having no experience in anything except painting, he decided to try his hand at real estate. He became a real estate agent and within one year was one of the top 10 agents in the country. He was loving life.

Then his past came back to haunt him. While he was running a very successful paint business, he knew nothing about taxes, and things of that nature. The IRS determined that he owed a huge amount in personal income taxes and his income was garnished. Because his wife was a stay-at-home mom, she was not able to make the amount of money needed to stay above water and as a result, he lost his house in foreclosure. Along the way, he went through a divorce, as well.

Having gone through such a tough time, he began to help other homeowners who were in foreclosure. He knew how they felt and wanted to help. He took his real estate business and turned it around to help homeowners in distress. When I met Bill he was a single dad, raising his two kids, and he was helping people who were in foreclosure. I was impressed and I appreciated what he had been through because, unknown to him, I had been through a similar situation.

I was married with an eight-month-old daughter when I found myself suddenly single. I had $75 in my purse, no car, no job, and no formal education. In addition, I was an emotional wreck. Life seemed hopeless. I realized that I had to do something to support my daughter and day care was not an option. I looked around for a while and, like Bill, I ended up in real estate. My avenue was a little different than his. I did not become a real estate agent, I became a "rehabber." I would find homeowners who were facing foreclosure, buy their house

FIGURE I.1   Family Photo

before they lost it to the bank, fix it up, and then sell it. Because of my lack of knowledge about the real estate industry, I made some serious mistakes and ended up losing a house in foreclosure. It was a very tough lesson and helped me truly understand what the people I was trying to help were really going through. It was a turning point in my life.

Several years later Bill and I met, fell in love, and married. We were now a happy family of five who have a heart for people in trouble. We turned our personal failures and desire to help others into a business. We began to empower homeowners by teaching them what they could do to help themselves. There is nothing more powerful than knowledge. Many homeowners have no idea what their rights are, what they can do themselves, and how to begin again. We are living proof that life will get better. Your best days are yet to come.

As you read this book, we will share some of the real life situations we faced and how we overcame them and how you can, too. Our goal is to show you that this, too, shall pass and that life will be great again. God has blessed us more than we could possibly imagine. We never imagined that we would be empowering others and sharing our personal problems with the world. To this day, it is still embarrassing to reveal our past to others, but it is necessary in order to best serve you. The Bible says that what the enemy means for harm—God will use for good. This is our "good" and we could not be happier.

ACKNOWLEDGMENTS

We'd like to thank Jesus for bringing us together and for giving us this opportunity to make a difference in your life.

We have been so incredibly blessed to have found each other and to be able to do what we love—spend time with each other, our kids, our family, our friends, and now—you.

PART I

Options for "Underwater" Property Owners

CHAPTER 1

Is Your Home Worth Less Than the Mortgage?

Because of the decline in home values in the United States, many properties today are worth the same as or less than the mortgage amount. Property values have fallen as much as 30 percent in some areas of the country. They are expected to continue to decline. Once the dust settles, we could be looking at a nationwide drop as high as 50 percent.

If you owe more than your house is worth and need to sell, you are what we consider to be "underwater." What do you do? The great news is that we have many options for you. Having a house that is underwater is not the end of the world. In the past, you might lose an underwater property in a foreclosure. That is not necessarily true today.

With the real estate market as crazy as it is now, your best option is usually working directly with your bank to get your house sold quickly. Because of the nationwide mortgage crisis, banks are bending over backward to help you get your house sold or to modify your loan because they don't want you to go into foreclosure. Banks don't like to foreclose for a number of reasons, including the fact that the foreclosure process itself is very expensive for them.

Let's look at a typical scenario for an underwater home-owner:

> You bought a house for $200,000 and borrowed $200,000.
> Property values dropped 30 percent.

➤ Your property is now worth $140,000.

➤ You still owe $190,000.

There are many reasons you may have for selling your property:

➤ You may be facing financial hardship.

➤ You have been transferred to another city and need to move.

➤ You are going through a divorce and need to sell quickly.

➤ Your spouse passed away and you can't bear the memories.

➤ You want to upgrade to a better neighborhood.

➤ You want to sell what you have and buy investment properties.

➤ You want to live closer to family.

How to Estimate the Value of Your Home

If you think your home may be "underwater" the first step is to get the best possible estimate of the current value of your property. To do this, you will need to find the actual selling price of similar houses in your immediate neighborhood in recent months. (These sales prices and the details on the sold homes, such as square footage, number of bedrooms, and other information about the property are called "comps.") When "pulling comps" (the term used by people in the real estate business), it is important to look at other properties similar to yours in size, number of bedrooms and bathrooms, age, and condition. If your property is a three bedroom, $1\frac{1}{2}$ bath; it would be worth less than a four bedroom, $2\frac{1}{2}$ bath property in the same neighborhood. Most people believe that only a real estate agent can look at comparable sales. Not true! Anyone can and we can help you. There are two types of comparable sales:

1. Properties that sold through the Multiple Listing Service (MLS).
2. Properties that did not sell through the MLS.

The MLS is available exclusively to real estate agents. Typically properties sold through the MLS were sold for a higher amount than properties sold by homeowners themselves. We prefer to pull comps from another source because the MLS often gives prices that don't consider the seller concessions. Seller concessions are things that the sellers throw into the transaction that increases the purchase price (for example, chandeliers, appliances, lawn equipment). Homeowners might also sell a property for $100,000 in the MLS because they have to pay 6 percent commission—$6,000. The same homeowners could sell their property for $94,000 themselves and save the commission.

There is a great web site that is available to the general public that we love to use—www.zillow.com. Our favorite feature of Zillow is that it is FREE. To pull comps, simply type in your property address, bedrooms, bathrooms, year built, and see what pops up. Zillow will show you properties within your subdivision, within one square mile, and within three square miles. When looking at comps, we try to find properties in the same subdivision. These will be the most accurate. We also look for properties that have sold in the past six months. However, with property values falling as fast as they are, we recommend looking at properties that have sold in the past three months if possible.

Another great feature of Zillow is that it prints out an area map. You can actually see your property in relation to the other properties you are looking at. If you see a property that sold on the same street as your property, it would be an ideal comp provided the property has about the same square footage as well as bedrooms and bathrooms. We look for properties that were distressed as well. It is not always possible to tell if the property was a distress sale or not. Some comp services will put information like special warranty deed, forced sale, foreclosure, or something along those lines. The type of deed used to transfer title or ownership often shows distress. If you see anything other than "warranty deed" or "quitclaim deed" it was most likely some form of distress.

Many homeowners or investors call real estate agents for help when trying to determine their property value. Real estate agents typically tell you what your property is worth based on what other properties are listed for. Listed prices have nothing to do with sold prices. You could have a house that was listed for $150,000 and sold for $125,000—$125,000 is the actual value. Agents typically list properties at the "top of the market." That is, they list properties for the highest amount possible and negotiate down from there. In this book, we want to help you deal with the reality of what your property is worth right now, in this market.

What Banks Want

Banks look at properties one of two ways:

1. Performing asset.
2. Nonperforming asset.

If your payments are on time, regardless of the property value, it is considered a performing asset. If your payments are late, regardless of the property value, it is considered a nonperforming asset. The banks realize that if homeowners can't sell their properties in this market, they might simply walk away—leaving the banks with the underwater property. Banks are in the business of lending money, not owning properties. So they may be willing to work with you in a number of ways we'll describe in this book to make it possible for you to sell your home for less than the mortgage, lower your payments so you can keep your house, or pursue another solution.

Here are some principles to help you understand why a bank may be willing to help you sell your underwater home:

> ➤ Banks are in the business of lending money, not owning houses.

➤ Banks have to carry a "loan loss reserve" against defaulting loans—this is a cash reserve of unlendable money the bank must hold while a property is in default.

➤ Banks have quarterly reports due to investors and shareholders that need to show profits.

➤ Banks have year-end reports due that need to show yearly profits or losses.

➤ Too many bad loans make it difficult for banks to borrow money to relend.

➤ Too many defaulted loans cause the banks stock to drop and investors to bail out.

➤ Too many defaulted loans cause banks to lay-off employees.

➤ Too many defaulted loans cause the bank to be absorbed by a bigger bank.

Basically, too many defaulted mortgage loans wreak havoc on the bank. For all these reasons, most banks would rather help you get your property sold than risk getting stuck with the property.

In this book, we are going to cover the most creative ways to get your property sold. We are also going to explain in depth the most important concept for underwater homeowners—the short sale.

Introduction to a Short Sale

A *short sale* will be one of your best options. Basically, you negotiate with the bank to accept less than what is owed as a full mortgage payoff. Using the previous example—you owe $190,000 on your house and it is only worth $140,000 in today's market. You are underwater. You put the house on the market using the techniques in this book and get an offer. The offer is $140,000. You contact the bank (using our step-by-step instruction) and get the bank to accept the $140,000 as full payment. You are able to sell the property and the bank does not get stuck with it if you decide to walk away. It creates a win/win solution for both of you.

In the past, your property had to be behind in payments or in foreclosure for the bank to consider a short sale. Because homeowners are walking away from properties in record numbers, banks are doing short sales on properties where the payments are not yet late. It is an amazing time in the real estate market. There are things happening that we have not seen in the past.

Other Options for Underwater Homeowners

Sometimes a bank will not agree to a short sale, or not until certain conditions are met. In this case, you will need to pursue other solutions we cover later in the book.

A short sale is the best option if you want to sell and your property is underwater. The other options we discuss involve you staying put. For example, you could do a loan modification. Loan modifications are actually simple to do. The bank has you fill out financial papers showing that your income has changed, that your property is worth less than you owe, or that you can no longer afford the payment. Once you prove it, the bank modifies or changes your payment. When doing a loan modification, the foreclosure is withdrawn. In some cases, you can actually lower your loan balance. Loan modifications are great options for homeowners or investors who got caught up in the interest-only craze where the reset payment is now unaffordable.

If the bank will not approve a loan modification, you could negotiate a forbearance agreement. A forbearance agreement is not an option unless your mortgage payments are behind. The bank works out a repayment plan that allows you to keep your property. The delinquent amount will be added to your current payment often making the agreement impossible to keep. If your current payment is $1,000 and you are $3,000 behind in mortgage payments, the bank may agree to spread the $3,000 over 12 equal payments. This means it would add $250 to your current payment of $1,000 dollars. Your new payment is $1,250. If $1,000 was difficult to pay, $1,250 might be impossible. When doing a forbearance agreement you remain in foreclosure until you make the 12th payment.

Some of you may be facing foreclosure, are fed up with the situation, and just want to walk away. In this case, a deed in lieu of foreclosure might be your best bet. You simply contact the bank and inform them that you are going to deed the property back to the bank instead of going through the foreclosure process. The banks hate this and will try very hard to work something else out with you. We recently contacted Country-Wide Home Loans to help a homeowner with a deed in lieu of foreclosure. (See Chapter 2 before you try this.) The bank immediately offered to accept a short sale, asked us to list the property for 90 days, and stated that they would take any decent offer. They also agreed to stop any proceedings while we waited out the 90 days. When the bank offered the short sale, we played dumb and let the bank rep explain it to us. The rep actually had a good grasp on what needed to be done in order to close a short sale. The bottom line was that the bank rep said that the bank did not want the house and would wait until we got an offer. We were thrilled!

We will also talk about trying to sell your home retail, renting it out to ride out the storm, and much more. Having an underwater property is never easy. We buy our house expecting the value to climb so that we can sell it later and move up to a bigger house. Unfortunately, it does not always work out like that. Who knew the market would change so dramatically, that property values would fall so fast, that most of America would be underwater. The great news is—there is a solution that will work for you . . . keep reading.

CHAPTER 2

What Happens If I Walk Away from My Property?

Stop Making Payments, Move Out, Let the Bank Foreclose

Most homeowners want to know what the consequences are if they simply walk away from a property, stop making payments, and let the bank foreclose on the property. You would be surprised how many people just walk away. The emotional stress is too great, the embarrassment is high, they can't deal with the constant phone calls, and they just move out. What happens then? Unfortunately, this is usually the worst option. We describe many better alternatives in this book.

If you stop making payments on your property and move out without negotiating anything with the bank, the bank will send someone to change the locks and secure the property:

- ➤ If you have a pool, the bank will cover it so neighborhood children don't fall in and drown.
- ➤ If it is winter, the bank will winterize the property.
- ➤ If the area is rough, the bank may board up the windows to prevent vandalism.
- ➤ The bank will usually put a note on the door stating that no one can trespass.

Basically, the bank will do whatever it takes to keep the property secure until it takes the property at the sheriff's sale and becomes the actual owner.

It is important to keep in mind that during this time, you *still* own the property and:

➤ You are *still* responsible if someone gets hurt on your property.

➤ You are *still* responsible if the house burns to the ground.

➤ You are *still* responsible if anything at all happens.

➤ It is *still* your house until the moment of the sheriff's sale.

Moving out and letting it go does not relieve you of your obligations, it just makes it easier on you emotionally not to have to deal with the daily stress. Personally, we'd be more worried about all the things that could happen by letting the property sit vacant.

One of our partners had a property she was trying to sell. The property was sitting vacant while it was on the market. Someone kept breaking into it and drinking, partying, having sex, doing drugs, urinating on the carpet, and more. Finally, our partner went to the neighbor next door and offered to pay him $500 dollars if he would call the police the next time vandals were in the house. A few days went by and the man noticed noise coming from the house and called the police. The police arrived and arrested the kids inside. Guess who it was. The neighbor's daughter and her friends! He was stunned and angry. The kids were arrested, sentenced, ended up with a criminal record, got probation, and had to pay restitution.

Bad things can happen to vacant homes. We have an investor friend who found a dead man in a vacant property. We went into another vacant house and it was full of loose pit bulls. Another had become the neighborhood crack house. There is no telling what can happen to a property while it sits vacant. If this is the option you choose, you need to at least keep insurance on the property. Unfortunately, if anyone gets hurt in your vacant house, *you* are responsible even if that person is committing an illegal act. Bottom line—you are fully responsible until the house becomes the possession of the bank.

If you are certain that you are just going to walk away, at least save as much money as possible before you leave. You will need a new place to rent and the new landlords will want first months' rent, last months' rent, and a security deposit, and they will do a credit check on you. When the new landlords see a fresh foreclosure, they might ask for a larger deposit. Try to prepare as much as possible before making a move.

Deed in Lieu of Foreclosure

Because walking away from a property leaves you liable until the bank forecloses, a smarter option might be to deed the house to the bank and relieve yourself of further responsibility. This option is called giving the bank a *Deed in Lieu of Foreclosure*. It's one of the first solutions your lender may offer when you tell him you're having trouble paying your mortgage. However, what the bank is offering you is good for the bank and not necessarily good for you. The bank wants you to deed the house to the bank, instead of (in lieu of) going through the foreclosure process because:

➤ It saves the bank a fortune in legal fees.
➤ After doing this, you can't file bankruptcy and buy time.
➤ The bank gets the bad debt off its books sooner.
➤ The bank does not have to follow the long foreclosure process.
➤ The bank gets ownership immediately.
➤ You move out immediately.

All of these end results are great for the bank. When speaking to a bank rep, the rep will make it sound as if this option is the perfect solution . . . it's easy, fast, won't cost you a thing. That is not true, it could cost you plenty.

Here is what the bank does not tell you:

➤ The bank could still place a foreclosure on your credit report.

➤ Once you deed the property back, the bank will sell it retail. Unless the bank makes a profit, it could sue you for its loss. This is called a "deficiency judgment."

➤ The bank may send you a 1099 showing its loss as income to you. Now you have an IRS problem, and may be expected to pay taxes on that "income."

➤ The market is down and it may take a year to sell your property. Suddenly you find out that you owe the bank $50,000 dollars because the bank lost money.

➤ Your credit could be affected because it might have a foreclosure on it and maybe a deficiency judgment, too.

We recently met with some homeowners who had an appointment the following morning to go to a title company and deed their house to the bank. The bank rep had talked them into a deed in lieu of foreclosure and had told them they would get a clean break from everything. We asked the homeowners if the bank rep had put everything in writing—that there would be no foreclosure and no deficiency judgment and no 1099. The bank rep had only made a verbal agreement and nothing was in writing. The homeowners were adamant about working with the bank. We wished them well and asked them to just do two small things before they signed—ask the bank rep to put in writing that the bank would not place a foreclosure on their credit and that the bank would not pursue a judgment if the bank sold the house later for a loss. The bank rep would not do either. The homeowners walked out and called us immediately stating that we were right—the bank was going to destroy the homeowners' credit.

How to Protect Yourself

Again, a deed in lieu is a great deal for the bank. It can be a good deal for you as well as long as you get everything in writing. A deed in lieu has no benefit to you at all unless the bank agrees, in writing:

➤ Not to pursue a deficiency judgment.

➤ Not to send a 1099.

➤ Not to place a foreclosure on your credit.

➤ To use the words—"paid in full" or "satisfied"—on your credit report.

If the bank will not agree to these terms, all you are doing is saving the bank a bunch of money in the foreclosure process. It does save you the emotional hassle of going through the foreclosure process, but you still have a foreclosure placed on your credit. The financial recovery time is the same.

Typically, the bank will use the words "friendly foreclosure" on your credit report. You might be just three payments late and the bank has not even filed a foreclosure yet. You agree to deed your house to the bank to avoid foreclosure only to find the words "friendly foreclosure" on your credit report months later. To top it off, you now find out that you still owe the bank money. You weren't even in foreclosure in the first place and still had plenty of options. Now your options are gone and you are much worse off than before. We are only fans of a deed in lieu if everything protecting you is in writing. Then it is a good option because it saves you months of emotional hassle, you don't have to deal with nasty letters and relentless calls from the bank, and you can start over faster and fresher.

If you own several properties and choose to do a deed in lieu, make sure you get the listed stipulations in writing for each property. New deed, new deal!

Your Losses Don't Stop with Foreclosure

Most homeowners we speak to believe that once their house is lost to the foreclosure process, they are off the hook. Not true—if the bank loses money (whether through a foreclosure or a short sale), it chases the homeowners for the loss through one (and only one) of two ways—a deficiency judgment or a 1099. Not only did the homeowners lose their house to the foreclosure process, they still owe the bank money. Both of these options allow the banks to write the loss off, but a deficiency judgment or a 1099 leave the homeowners in a worse situation than they were before. If you own several rentals, you could really get hurt financially receiving several 1099s from the bank.

How Does This Work?

When a homeowner loses a house in the foreclosure process, the bank usually suffers a loss. Here is a typical example: The homeowners have a property worth $200,000; they owe $200,000 and are in foreclosure. The bank takes the house at the sheriff's sale and then sells it retail. After paying real estate commissions, attorney's fees, taxes, and other related costs, the banks nets $140,000. The bank suffered a $60,000 loss.

The same holds true for a short sale, which we discuss in Part II. You get the bank to accept $140,000 on a $200,000 property and the bank still loses $60,000. Even though the bank accepted the short sale, it still needs to write off the loss. Banks do that by pursuing a deficiency judgment or sending you a 1099. (When we negotiate a short sale for a homeowner or another investor, we ask the bank to waive both.)

There are several bills that have been put in place by Congress to relieve homeowners of any further tax liability be-cause of a foreclosure. The problem with these bills is that they are not permanent. We have a blog—www.theieu.com where we keep you posted with up-to-the-minute information. Since you will be reading this book at different times of the year, check the blog to see what legislation is in place. There is cur-rently a bill in place that does not allow the banks to seek a deficiency or a 1099. It is a great bill, *if you qualify*. Congress reviews this bill every few Decembers so there is no telling how long it will be in place. In Chapter 6, we list many sites to visit to see what is happening currently in Congress.

Assuming that you do not qualify for an exemption, you would then receive a deficiency judgment or a 1099. Let's take a moment to review each of these and how they might affect you.

Deficiency Judgment

Deficiency judgments vary by state. For example, in California a bank cannot pursue a deficiency judgment on a purchase mortgage. It can, however, pursue a deficiency judgment if the homeowner refinanced the property and obtained a new first mortgage. There are other states with similar laws. The best way to determine what is happening in your state is to ask a real estate attorney. If you are struggling with payments or have an underwater property, it is always best to consult with an attorney before you take any action. Even though we are giving you our best opinion, we are not attorneys and can't give legal advice. There are many attorneys who offer free consultations. Most of these attorneys will advise you to file for bankruptcy and will ask for money up-front. This is one option. Consider all of your options before making a decision. Every option we are covering in this book can be done by you without an attorney. Meet with an attorney, ask questions about current laws regarding deficiencies and 1099s and take notes. If you get the bank to waive both, the consultation will not be necessary.

To fully understand a deficiency, let's use the earlier example. We'll assume the bank lost $60,000 (either by foreclosure or short sale). It would then turn your file over to a collection company or an attorney who would sue you for the loss. If you did not pay the balance, the collection company would get a judgment against you and that judgment would then be placed on your credit report against your social security number. You can't buy another house until this judgment is paid off. It can stay on your credit report for up to 10 years. Once the collection company gets the judgment, you could call and short sale the judgment; however, that would still mean you have to come up with a large amount of cash.

When negotiating the short sale, ask the bank to waive its right to a deficiency judgment. More often than not, the bank will waive its right to a deficiency judgment if you can prove a solid hardship.

Most of you probably don't care about the 1099 or deficiency judgment right now. Your main concern is what to do "today" to move on. However, in a few years you will care so let's deal with it now.

It's important for you to know that the lender cannot pursue a deficiency judgment *and* issue a 1099.

Because the bank is **writing off** the loss on its books, it can only write it off once. If the bank sent a 1099 and then pursued a deficiency—it would be writing the loss off twice. If the bank agrees to waive the deficiency judgment or waive the 1099, get it in writing. If the loss mitigation rep verbally agrees and then forgets to send a "waiver of deficiency" or a "waiver of 1099" with the closing papers, guess what? The bank could still pursue one or the other. **IT MUST BE IN WRITING.**

If the bank does give you a deficiency judgment, it can be wiped out with a Chapter 7 bankruptcy. If you are thinking of filing bankruptcy anyway, it is not a bad idea to ask the bank for the deficiency judgment so that your attorney can list it with your other debt and wipe it out.

We are not huge advocates of bankruptcy; however, there are times when bankruptcy makes sense. If you have thousands of dollars in credit card debt and a huge deficiency judgment hanging over your head, bankruptcy might be the right move for you. An attorney can give you the proper advice. Always consult an attorney if filing for bankruptcy.

The 1099 Tax Monster

Banks issue 1099s as another way to write off losses. Using the same example as above, the bank suffered a $60,000 loss. It sends you a 1099 that shows you **earned** $60,000 in income. Since you did not actually earn the $60,000 you have no extra money to pay the taxes. You're already in foreclosure and now you owe income taxes on an extra $60,000. Having a potential IRS issue can add to your current stress.

Let's say that you received a 1099 for the $60,000. That might put you in the 30 percent tax bracket this year. Now you might owe the IRS $18,000 in income taxes. If you have ever dealt with the IRS, you know that if you don't pay the taxes on time, penalties begin to accrue—fast. In no time, you owe double that amount—$36,000—and now the IRS investigates you. It can spiral out of control fast.

The best way to deal with a 1099 is to consult a tax accountant and see what can be worked out. In many cases, you might not owe anything. An accountant may be able to file "insolvency" or get a "one-time homeowners exemption" or use your "adjusted basis" for write-offs. If you qualify for any of these, you would be off the hook.

If you suffered loss in income, are going through a divorce, had a mortgage payment that reset to an unaffordable payment, or anything along those lines, you may qualify for insolvency. You are considered insolvent when your total liabilities exceed your total assets. It is not that difficult to qualify for insolvency when you have had a foreclosure and it may be a perfect solution to your problem. Remember, we are always going to ask the bank to waive the 1099 (in writing); this is a worst-case scenario.

If you lost your property in foreclosure or short sale, and you did $40,000 worth of work on it (and had receipts to prove it), the IRS would take the $40,000 off your taxes against the $60,000 you owe and you'd owe taxes on just $20,000—this is a sample of what "adjusted basis" means.

As you can see, there are many options when receiving a 1099. This is why you **must** use a tax accountant to file your taxes the first year after losing a property in distress. If you simply sell your house for a profit, then you would owe taxes on the profit earned. It is still a good idea to work with an accountant because you may have adjusted basis write-offs that you are not aware of.

Mortgage Forgiveness Debt Relief Act

In the next section, we are going to discuss some of the new government acts. Again, check with a tax accountant to see which of these you qualify for.

To see what exemptions you qualify for, check out the following sites:

➤ www.irs.gov.
➤ www.whitehouse.gov.

➤ www.govtrack.us.

➤ www.sccgov.org.

We found the following information on the www.irs.gov web site very helpful.

President Bush signed the Mortgage Forgiveness Debt Relief Act on December 20, 2007. The purpose of the bill is to help homeowners who are caught in the housing crisis. This bill is not permanent and will be reviewed in a few years. If the housing crisis is under control, the bill will be taken off the books. If not, it may change or stay on the books on a year-by-year basis.

What Is the Mortgage Forgiveness Debt Relief Act of 2007?

The act allows you to walk away from a foreclosure free and clear. The bank forgives the potential income you would get with a 1099. It is meant to be used on your primary residence so it will not help an investor with multiple properties.

What Does That Mean?

When the bank accepts a short sale or sells your property for a loss and sends you a 1099, you are supposed to claim this income on your tax returns. When claiming this as income, the new act allows the debt to be forgiven—meaning you don't owe taxes on it. This is an amazing statute. There has never been anything quite like it before. So, if you have to lose your house, now is a good time because you can truly start over.

Does the Mortgage Forgiveness Debt Relief Act of 2007 Apply to All Forgiven or Canceled Debts?

No, the act applies to your primary residence only. Again, anyone with multiple properties will not qualify for this exclusion.

What about Refinanced Homes?

The act applies to properties that have been refinanced with some exceptions. You can only be forgiven the original amount of the loan. For example, you have a property where you owed $150,000 and then you refinanced it for $200,000, pulling out $50,000 profit. Only the original amount of $150,000 would qualify under the new act. If the bank sold the house for $125,000, $25,000 would be exempt and you could be sent a 1099 for the $50,000 that you pulled out of the house. It is considered profit even though you lost the house to foreclosure.

Does This Provision Apply for the 2007 Tax Year Only?

Currently, this bill will apply to the 2007, 2008, and 2009 tax years. Once it is reviewed, it might stay in place longer. In the current market, walking away from a house is a solid option because you can be forgiven the debt. In the past, most homeowners suffered a deficiency or a 1099.

If the Forgiven Debt Is Excluded from Income, Do I Have to Report It on My Tax Return?

Absolutely. You must report the amount of the debt. As we said earlier, it is important to use a tax accountant to file your taxes the first year after a foreclosure or deed in lieu. You will use Form 982 and attach it to your tax return.

Where Can I Get This Form?

You can download the form at www.irs.gov or call (800) 829-3676. If you call to order, allow 7 to 10 days for delivery.

How Do I Know or Find out How Much Was Forgiven?

The bank will send you a Form 1099—C, Cancellation of Debt by January 31. The forgiven amount will show in box 2. Again, do not attempt to file your own taxes the first year. You don't want to miss any write-offs that you might qualify for and you certainly don't want to make a mistake and owe unknown taxes. It will eventually catch up with you and you could find yourself under a major investigation—talk about stress!

Can I Exclude Debt Forgiven on My Second Home, Credit Card, or Car Loans?

This bill is meant for use on primary residence only—not credit cards, second homes, or investment properties . . . sorry.

If part of the forgiven debt doesn't qualify for exclusion from income under this provision, is it possible that it may qualify for exclusion under a different provision?

Absolutely, as we mentioned before, you may qualify as insolvent. You would need an accountant to help you with this.

Is there a limit on the amount of forgiven qualified principal residence indebtedness that can be excluded from income?

There is no dollar limit if the principal balance of the loan was less than $2 million ($1 million if married filing separately for the tax year) at the time the loan was forgiven.

We hope this helps you to understand what the government is doing to try to help. It would be nice if these laws became permanent so that distressed homeowners could walk away and truly get a fresh start. Financial hardship is so stressful to begin with—adding possible tax issues makes it much worse.

You may be reading this book in 2009 or 2012. The Acts that were put into place change with the economy. Again, check out the web sites listed earlier to see what is going on today. Some of this information changed even while we were writing the book.

CHAPTER 3

If You Are in Financial Trouble, Deal with Your Emotions First!

Whether you are an investor or a homeowner, admitting and facing that you are in trouble is extremely difficult to do. We explained in the introduction how people get into trouble. Having worked with so many homeowners and investors in foreclosure as well as having been in trouble ourselves, we honestly can say that we know how you feel. There are many emotions that come along with financial hardship . . . anger, denial, fear, depression, and embarrassment.

It is difficult to admit that you might have failed, made such a bad decision, gotten into financial trouble, have to rely on others, have to ask family members (or friends) for help, let your family down, have to move the kids, and many more negative feelings.

Where do you start? The best way to accept that you are in trouble is to deal with and recognize your emotions, why you have them, and how you can get rid of them.

The Typical Mindset of People in Distress

Everyone involved with a foreclosure has strong emotions:

> **As an investor,** it is important to learn which mindset a homeowner is in so that you can help them.

➤ **As a homeowner,** it is important to recognize what mindset you are in for you to move on.

As an investor in trouble, it is important to recognize where you might be and what other investors are thinking when they offer to help. Let's discuss some of the emotions you may be experiencing.

Denial

Denial is probably the hardest emotion to overcome. When people (or investors who saw your name in the foreclosure filings) ask you what is going on, how they can help, is everything okay because you seem tense, why you are moving, you say things like:

➤ I've already taken care of it.
➤ I'm listing my house with a Realtor.
➤ I hired an attorney.
➤ I'm going to refinance and pull out some cash.
➤ I'm working with a mortgage broker.
➤ I made up the back payments.
➤ The bank has the wrong house.
➤ Don't worry about it, we're fine.
➤ I have no idea what you are talking about.

When people ask you how you got into trouble, you blame everyone else or deny the problem altogether. It is normal to feel denial. It takes time to process what is happening.

We believe that investors have a harder time with denial than homeowners do because they are supposed to be buying and selling houses for a profit. They are supposed to be helping other people in distress, not be in it themselves. They cannot have their competition see their name in the paper. The competition will tell the homeowners in distress that the investor trying to help them is in foreclosure himself. When an investor's name goes in the paper, it's almost a death sentence to his investing career for a while. Unfortunately, his competition will use this to their advantage for as long as they can.

When the market was going crazy and property values were going up at record speed, many people decided to try their hand at investing. Unfortunately, most people didn't take time to get the proper investing education and ended up in trouble while trying to gain wealth. It can be very difficult to come back from that. You might be skittish next time around or decide to give up. Remember, Henry Ford went bankrupt five times. Never quit!

Anger

Anger is typically the next emotion. You have accepted the fact that you are facing financial hardship and are mad at the world because of it.

When people (or investors who saw your name in the foreclosure files) ask you what is going on or what they can do to help, you say things like:

- Get off my property.
- Stay away from here.
- I'll call the cops.
- You're such a jerk coming to my house.
- Stop bothering me.
- Who do you think you are getting into my personal business.

Typically with anger, you respond in an argumentative manner whenever anyone tries to find out what is happening. Deep inside you are mad at the world as well as being terribly embarrassed over things. Anger is just embarrassment on steroids. As with denial, it is common to go from one emotion to the next. You may feel anger for a while, then you figure out a possible solution, it falls apart, and—bam—the anger comes back.

You see neighbors or family members who seem to have everything going in their direction and you feel angry about it—"Why are you having all these problems and they aren't; you're a good person, why is this happening to you"—it is completely normal to have these feelings. That's why they call it anger. Whatever you do, if you are married, don't start blaming your spouse whether it's their fault or not. It will not help your situation; it can only make it worse. Take comfort in knowing that this too shall pass.

Fear

Fear might be the next emotion you experience. You lay awake at night wondering what you will do, where you will go, what will happen to your credit, will your marriage survive, why you bought those properties in the first place, and many more fearful worries.

When people ask you what happened (or an investor shows up at your door because of the foreclosure notice), you say things like:

> ➤ I'm in so much trouble.
> ➤ The impact of this foreclosure is just killing me.
> ➤ I don't know what I'm going to do.
> ➤ Thank God you're here.
> ➤ Thank you for working with me.
> ➤ I can't sleep at night.
> ➤ I don't know what will happen to my kids.
> ➤ If I lose this house, how will I ever buy another house.

While you are in the fearful mode, life may seem scary. As with all the other emotions, this one will pass as well. The great things about dealing with all your feelings is that once you accept them, you can start working toward a solution.

Depression

Depression is one of the toughest emotions to overcome. Depression can cause people to take drastic measures—we have even seen people commit suicide. Remember, this is only a house . . . not a family member who is dying. You must start letting go of the emotional attachment to it. Once the emotional attachment is gone, life will get easy again and start going in the right direction. There is life after foreclosure, after losing something that was important to you, after losing a business, after all things—there is a new life waiting for you.

While feeling depressed you might say and think things like:

> ➤ I'm in a hopeless situation.
> ➤ I've tried everything and nothing works.
> ➤ What do you think you can do to help? Nothing is working.
> ➤ Other investors have tried.
> ➤ My life and family are ruined.
> ➤ I'm so screwed up.
> ➤ I'm such a loser.
> ➤ How will I ever face people again?
> ➤ I'm a good person; why is this happening to me?
> ➤ I didn't do anything to deserve this.

Embarrassment

Embarrassment is common to have throughout the entire process. You might feel anger for a while, then you'll be embarrassed again, then in denial, then embarrassed again, then angry, and then back to embarrassment.

We have all been in embarrassing situations before and no matter how many people help or how you resolve the situation, the fact that you were in it is embarrassing forever. We still get embarrassed (to a much smaller scale) talking about it and now we are sharing our personal situation with the world by writing this book. Talk about embarrassing! It's kind of scary to know that your personal secrets are going to be exposed and for sale is every bookstore in the United States.

We're sure that some people will judge us while others will look at what we have been through and who and what we have become today and it will give them hope. God has placed it on both of our hearts to share and help others to make a difference in their lives. Many of you don't have family or resources, so we hope to be the person who helps you start over and begin a new, better, more exciting life.

Here are some of the feelings you might experience and some of the things you may say or think during the embarrassment phase:

➤ My kids will have to change schools and people might figure out why we moved.

➤ Hope my neighbors don't find out about this.

➤ How did you find this out?

➤ Who else knows?

➤ Please don't park your car with those "I Buy Houses Signs" on it in front of my house.

➤ Please come in . . . hurry.

➤ What do you mean this is public record?

➤ What if my boss/family/friends find out?

➤ Every investor in town knows I am in trouble and I won't be able to get back into the business later.

➤ What will people think of me as a person, mom, dad, or provider?

As with the rest of the feelings, embarrassment will soon fade and that is when you can start dealing with what is happening to you and move on.

It is important to understand that harboring any type of negative feelings can result in many physical symptoms—lack of sleep, short temperedness, high blood pressure, heart attacks, strokes, anxiety attacks, break outs, loss of hair, and so many more things. Please don't let stress and anger get the best of you. Trust us, someday you will look back on this as a learning experience. Maybe not for a while, but someday . . . what doesn't kill you makes you stronger. Remember God won't give you more than you can handle. No matter how tough things are—you can handle it and start over.

Acceptance

Acceptance is the emotion to work toward. Once you have fully accepted your situation, you can really make things happen. You know you are in acceptance when you stop losing sleep, work diligently toward a solution, aren't so mortified to talk about your situation, are beginning to accept advice and help from others, actually look forward to moving and starting over, begin to realize that you can invest again, know that people aren't judging you and talking about you, stop feeling paranoid, and so on. It is a great day when acceptance sets in.

When acceptance sets it, don't become complacent. Keep the ball rolling in the right direction.

How It Feels to Be Trapped

There is not a worse feeling in the world than the pressure of financial hardship. We have both experienced hardship in the past.

Dwan's Story

When my daughter was just eight months old, her dad left. I had $75 in my purse and no husband, no car, no job, and was completely shocked. I spent several days in my apartment crying and trying to muster the courage to call my parents and tell them. I was humiliated, embarrassed, freaked-out, sick to my stomach, worried how I was going to care for this child . . . did I mention embarrassed?

I didn't want to ask for help because I had been on my own since I was 18. I was now 30 and penniless. I took pride in the fact that at 18 I lived on my own, had a nice apartment, had a fast car, made good money, and was independent. My parents raised me to be independent and strong. My dad always said I could do anything. Now, I had to tuck my tail between my legs and ask for help. I can't think of a more depressing time in my entire life.

Once I worked up the courage to call my parents, it stunned me how my family came out of the woodwork to help. I was expecting a lecture; instead, I received nothing but love and support. My aunt lent me money for a car, my mom bought groceries and helped babysit, my dad and sister bought Ayla school clothes . . . everyone helped. It was amazing.

What started out as a nightmare turned into a major blessing. Everyone supported me during this difficult time. The best part is, I found real estate and have been doing it ever since. I love to help others. Because I personally experienced such a difficult time myself, I have a heart for people in trouble. I know exactly where you are coming from and I feel blessed to be in your life to help you get a fresh start.

My family has always been close, but my dilemma made us even closer and we have stayed that way. There are people who will be happy to help and support you if you'll just let them.

Bill's Story

I grew up working for my dad who was a paint contractor. In my 20s, I branched out and started my own company. I had a wife, a huge house in Texas, two small kids, 50 employees, drove a Mercedes, had a live-in housekeeper, an indoor swimming pool, and was living life to the fullest.

Unfortunately, I didn't know much about running a big business, having the proper paperwork, how to do my own books, the benefits of an accountant, or anything else I needed to know to run such a large and profitable business. Eventually the IRS caught up with me and I had been doing everything wrong. My dad had run a very small company and took care of everything himself and I didn't realize that the other side of the business existed. I sold my business and moved to Colorado.

When I got to Colorado, I built a mansion in the mountains, and became a successful real estate agent. After many meetings with the IRS about my past paint business, I owed hundreds of thousands of dollars in taxes.

Long story short—I had my wages garnished. Because I had high living expenses, my wife was unable to earn enough to keep up our lifestyle and we lost everything. I went through a bankruptcy and a foreclosure and lost my house, my car, and eventually, my wife. I did get to keep the kids though.

Want to hear how sad it got—the bank kicked us out of our house on Christmas Eve. Couldn't they have waited until the day after Christmas? It was the lowest point in my life. We loaded up the kids, our pets, and the Christmas presents and went, tails tucked, to a friend's house. I could not have been more embarrassed, humiliated, devastated, feeling like a complete loser and failure as a man—utter devastation had fallen on my head. I couldn't even see light at the end of the tunnel.

During the time my wages were garnished, I helped a family in foreclosure. Because I had just gone through one, I knew quite a bit about the system. I was able to help these people keep their house and my life as an investor began.

Like Dwan, I love to help people because I know where they are coming from. The lowest point in my life was during those years.

Look at us now—in love, we have great kids, money, and the ability to help others for a living; it is amazing that we came from where we were then to where we are now. We both really believe that what doesn't kill you will make you stronger. As we said before, God will not give you more than you can handle. Keep that in mind.

We often wonder if we would have gotten into the business of helping others had we not both had trouble ourselves. Our own problems made us strong and gave us both a desire to give back. Maybe the problems you are facing today will become a blessing down the road. It is often difficult to step back and look at a bad time as a positive experience, but good things do come from bad.

So stop staying awake at night wondering what you are going to do. Look for the silver lining and move on.

Putting Your Pride Aside—The First Step to a New Life

The very first step to a new life is to put your pride aside. You may be the first one in your family to go through a hard time. You may think you are the only one in your entire family going through a hard time. We'll bet there are others in your family and you just don't know about it because everyone keeps it quiet. You probably had people in your family who survived the Great Depression.

If you are an investor, this time is especially difficult. It's worse if you have people in your family who were not supportive of your career choice to begin with. We're sure you have already heard at least one "I told you so" from some supportive family member. Don't worry about it. How you handle adversity is a true test of who you are as a person.

The first step is to admit you have a problem and then take a few deep breaths and call your family together for an emergency meeting. This means sitting down with as many people as possible—face-to-face. People will be more inclined to help you when they see others helping. Explain what is happening and that you need help. If you have no way to continue making mortgage payments, don't ask for money to bail out of foreclosure. Ask for help to *start over.* Maybe you'll need to rent for a few years, pay off credit card debt, get your credit fixed, save for a rainy day. Trying to save your house is not the answer unless you can make the full payment—principal, interest, taxes, and insurance—with ease. Otherwise, you'll go further in debt and be right back where you are today.

If you are an investor, call the bank and see what its policy is on deeding back the properties or doing a short sale—both topics that we will discuss in detail soon. Deeding property back may save you the hassle of going through foreclosure, it stops all the nasty collection calls, and can make your life easier. It is very difficult to make the initial call, but please do it. Your life will immediately feel lighter and peace will start to set in. It is the first step to taking control.

Starting over is VERY difficult to do. Ask yourself why—it all points back to our pride. We don't want people to know we are struggling, that we can't pay our bills, or that we made some bad decisions. Why? Look at the worst-case scenario—you tell someone you are in trouble and ask for help and they say no. Are you any worse off? No, you're not. Once you tell the first person, it gets easier...trust us...we know from personal experience.

In fact, now we tell people all the time because it turned out to be the beginning of an amazing life for both of us—together. If anyone looks at us differently because of our past, we honestly could care less. Who is someone else to judge us? The old saying, "Don't judge a person unless you have walked a mile in their shoes," is so true. We have both walked a mile in your shoes, now we want you to walk a mile in ours.

Having been on both sides of the fence, we like this side better. Honestly though, we both feel that the other side made us better people. It is easy to have money, get caught up in your own life, and become complacent. Suffering through financial difficulty makes you a better person if you see the lesson. We were both very prideful, self-centered people, and did little to contribute to society. Neither of us supported charities, volunteered, helped elderly neighbors, tithed, or did much of anything for others.

Now we support several charities, volunteer our time to financial counseling, have given homeless families homes, have helped make mortgage payments for others, paid medical expenses, helped someone have an organ transplant, and so much more. Most everything we do, we do anonymously. People like to help and be recognized for it...why? It always goes back to the same thing—pride. We like being fussed-over because we did a good deed. It makes us feel good about ourselves. Start a new trend—help someone without telling *anyone* that you did it. It is an amazing feeling and it will help you heal through your own tough time...besides that, God will bless you for it.

Make it a point to start today. Look for people you can help in *any* small way.

How to Get Free from Your Property and Get on with Your Life

Sit down tonight and make a list of people who might be able to help you. This would include friends, family, bankers, the church, other investors, and neighbors. Remember, meet with these people in person—if possible.

You may need help with many things—money, groceries, house cleaning, car repairs, kids, and more:

> ➤ Someone could offer to watch your kids two nights a week while you work part time.
>
> ➤ Someone could clean your house while you work overtime or job hunt.
>
> ➤ Someone can pay for your first month's rent on an apartment or maybe co-sign on the lease with you.
>
> ➤ Someone can help you with dinner if you are overstressed.
>
> ➤ Someone can pay for or do a car repair so you can job hunt.
>
> ➤ Someone could babysit on a Saturday afternoon while you hold open houses to try and sell your investment properties before you give them back to the bank.

There are so many things friends and family will help you with if you just ask. Before you ask for help, you'll need to prepare by doing the following:

> ➤ Make a list of the money you owe—credit cards, late mortgage payments, late payments on anything else, list of rentals, and so on.
>
> ➤ Then make a list of fixed expenses. Stuff you must pay for on a monthly basis—rent, electric, phone, insurance, car payments, groceries, and so on.
>
> ➤ Put together a budget that you plan to stick to.
>
> ➤ Most importantly, make a list of what you will do different from today forward.

People like to help people who have a plan to move ahead. There is nothing worse than to help someone only to see them right back where they were before you gave up your hard-earned money to help.

Several years ago, we helped a neighborhood kid with some dental work after a major accident. His mother was a single mom, he had a terrible car accident, and her insurance didn't pay for dental work. He lost his front teeth and had broken others. We heard about it and went to a dentist, paid for the work and sent the boy there . . . no strings attached. We both have nice smiles and have worn braces and knew what it could do to a teenager's self-confidence to face life with wrecked teeth. Whenever we saw him, he would always run up and thank us. He is now out of high school and we saw him in the store the other day and he was buying chew—that nasty stuff that you chew and spit. It turns your teeth green, causes mouth cancer, and is extremely disgusting. We both felt so much disappointment. We thought, "Do you know how much money we have in that mouth and you're chewing snuff." Then we remembered that we did it with no strings attached and if he wants to rot out the beautiful, expensive teeth he has, it is not our business. The point—we helped because it was the right thing to do at the time and we did it with no strings attached . . . at all. This is what you need from the people who help you now—no strings attached.

During the family meeting, have your friends and family help you take a realistic look at your late payments, your credit card debt, your investment mistakes, and so on. Will you be better off to file bankruptcy and start over or work out a payment plan and stay put. We'll venture to guess it will be easier to get a fresh start. Again, it is not the end of the world to file bankruptcy or face a foreclosure and start over. The key to success is not to let it happen again. We are supposed to learn from our mistakes.

When you ask for help, it is important that anyone who gives you money, **gives** you the money. It is not a loan; it is a gift. The biggest thing to come between friends and family members is money. You don't want that person reminding you all the time that you owe them money. You are looking for a fresh start . . . it must be a gift that will never be brought up again. Your promise to them is that you will, in turn, help someone else down the road by giving them money when they are in need.

If you don't have family or friends who can help—and you know because you called a meeting, not that you were too embarrassed to ask—look other places. Churches, charities, temporary agencies all offer food, gas, emergency car payments, emergency electric and water bill payments, and many other things. They'll even give you clothes, pay for school supplies, pay for your kids to get shots, and so much more. It is typically harder to go to a charity because we think that only the poorest, homeless people go to these places. Not true. Many fine respectable people use these services. That's what they are for—emergencies. Please don't be embarrassed to ask for help.

Once you've gone over what you owe, what you must pay for, and what you must give up, and you have let it sink in for few days, it is time to take action. Let's look at some options you have.

CHAPTER 4

Aggressive First Steps to Get the Highest Possible Price

Let's talk about what to do if your property is in distress and then we'll cover what to do if it is not. Whether an investor or a homeowner in distress, selling your property is always going to be your best option. If it sells before the sheriff's sale (the foreclosure sale date), you won't have a final foreclosure on your credit report. Your credit report will reflect that a foreclosure was filed, but that it was solved before the final sale date. It does help your credit when starting over.

If you are an investor who owns several investment properties, selling them will help a lot. Of course, having 10 foreclosures is hard to recuperate from. You might be better filing bankruptcy and wiping the slate clean.

Let's cover aggressive ways to sell your property. If this does not work, you can try one of the many options we have for you—a short sale, deed in lieu, renting, and much more—so please keep reading.

Try to Sell the Property Yourself before Calling a Real Estate Agent

Before you call a real estate agent and list your house, try a few other options first:

- ➤ Place an ad on www.craigslist.com.
- ➤ Place an ad on www.ebay.com.

➤ Place an ad on www.loopnet.com.

➤ Place other ads on any "For Sale by Owner" (FSBO) site you can find.

If you have a $200,000 property, you could save $12,000 in real estate commission, which means you can sell the house for less. We suggest trying to sell your property yourself for 30 days. If you get no bites, consider listing it.

To determine what your house is worth, look on www.zillow.com for comparable sales. This is a free service that offers comps. Remember, you are facing hardship so sell the house for as low as possible to unload it. Now is not the time to get greedy and look to make a profit. Now is the time to move it as quickly as possible before you lose it.

Figure 4.1 shows a few sample ads that have worked well for us.

You pay for each line when running ads so abbreviate everything you can (see Figure 4.2). The goal is to put as much information in the ad as possible.

Look at ads in your local papers to get a feel for what they abbreviate. The person taking the ad should help with this. Most papers will allow you to place an ad and will bill you in 30 days. This helps cut immediate costs.

Notice in our ads we state "seller desperate" or "motivated seller" or something along those lines. This will cause your phone to ring. The more calls you get, the better your chances to sell your property quickly.

FIGURE 4.1   Sample Ads

2/1/cp. Seller desperate. Will pay cc. New w/d, c/h/a. 555-5555 $99K	4/1½/1. c/h/a. New everything. Motivated seller. Will pay cc. 555-5555 259K OBO	3/2/1. seller will pay costs. Newly remodeled. Need to sell. w/d/c/h/a. 349K 555-5555
Bring your toothbrush, 3/2 spotless & ready for your family $99,700 Desperate Seller! 555-5555	3/2 Dollhouse, needs nothing but your furniture. Seller will help. $57,400 555-5555. OBO	Low down, low monthly to qualified buyer. Seller will help. 2/1/1,fcd yd, fm rm. $69,900, 555-5555

FIGURE 4.2   Abbreviations

3/2/1cg = 3 bedroom, 2 bath, 1 car garage
2/1/cp = 2 bed, 1 bath, carport
4/1½/1 = 4 bed, one and a half baths, 1 car garage
fc yd = fenced yard
fm rm = family room
OBO = or best offer
CC = closing costs
w/d= washer/dryer
c/h/a= central, heat, and air

Don't be embarrassed to use these words in your ads. You want your phone to ring. Other people are always looking for a good deal and these words generate interest.

Always advertise your property as far below market as you can to sell it before the foreclosure goes any further.

If properties are selling for $150,000, sell yours for $129,900. Again, the goal is to sell your house as quickly as possible. The lower the price, the more buyers who will show interest. Even if you have 20 houses in your neighborhood that are for sale, do not let this intimidate you. Yours could be the perfect house for someone else and might sell the first day.

Using a Real Estate Agent

If, after 30 days of trying to sell it yourself, no one has shown any interest, consider listing the property with a real estate agent. Real estate agents will also run comps and give you their opinion of value, have you sign a listing agreement, and put it on the market. Since many people wanting to buy a house use an agent, it might prove worthwhile.

The downside to listing your house is that most people who use agents look for new listings. Once another 30 days has passed, your listing will be old and will get very little attention. Also, many agents take as many listings as possible just hoping that one will close and don't put much effort into the actual selling process. They rely on agents who show houses to sell their listings. You have listing agents and selling agents. Look for a selling agent.

Take time to interview an agent. Ask how many listings they took in the past six months and how many of their *own* listings they sold. If they took 25 listings and didn't sell any, your house won't sell either.

Many times a real estate agent can list your house and in the "special clauses" section of the listing agreement put the words—"Bank will accept a short sale. Bring all offers." The agent then takes any offer given and presents it to the bank. The bank will then decide either to accept or pass. Because of the millions of foreclosures that are predicted, banks are doing more and more short sales every day. We'll talk more about short sales in Part II.

You can use a real estate agent, like we mentioned earlier, and put key words in the listing agreement under special clauses. Use words like:

- TLC.
- Must sell.
- Desperate seller.
- Seller will help—this means you will pay some of the new buyer's closing costs.
- Too good to be true.
- $1,000 bonus to agent who brings a buyer before _____ (30 days or less from the listing agreement).
- Distressed seller.

Your listing agent should be able to help you with more key words. The point is to make it sound better than the other listings and to draw as much attention as possible.

If you are an investor who has multiple properties, use key words like:

- Investor must sell.
- Package deal available.
- Seller will pay closing costs.

➤ Will break up the package.

➤ Great cash flow possible.

➤ $3,000 bonus to agent who sells entire package.

➤ Investors in over their heads.

Whether distressed or not, we have one important tip—**Do not show your home.** What? Yeah, you read right—don't show your home, at least not the conventional way. Once it is listed in the MLS or on one of the web sites we mentioned—start taking phone calls. Tell everyone that you will show it at 1:00 on Saturday (or whatever time you want) and have everyone come at the same time. This will cause a buying frenzy and your house could sell in one day. If you are selling more than one property, hold open houses at different times.

We have used this technique many times with great success. When people see other people going after the same thing, it increases the desire to want to own it. People always want what others have. When potential buyers see 10 or 15 people looking at the same thing, suddenly it becomes more desirable.

Despite your best efforts, there are many reasons your house might not sell in time to beat the foreclosure sale:

➤ You owe more than your house is currently worth.

➤ It needs too much work to sell it retail.

➤ You are in one of the many areas that is very depressed.

➤ Industry is moving out of your area and there are no jobs.

If any of these situations apply to you, we have a possible solution—a short sale. We will talk about short sales in detail in Part II, but the gist of it is this:

A short sale is where you negotiate with the bank to accept less than what you owe against your property as full payment. For example, you have a house worth $100,000; you owe $100,000 and are facing foreclosure. You call the bank, ask them to do a short sale, they agree and they accept $60,000 as a full payoff. Now you can sell your house below market and get out of foreclosure. Banks will short sale investment properties, too.

What If My House Is Underwater but the Payments Aren't Late?

If your mortgage payments are current, you need to move, and you can't sell your house because of what you owe, so you have a tougher situation to deal with. Try the options we mentioned earlier to aggressively sell the property. If it does not work, you are going to have to contact the bank and try to work something out. You can't sell a property for less than you owe unless the bank agrees. Clear title can't be passed so you must work with the bank.

If the bank sees that you have a good job, solid income, are not behind on payments, and simply want to move, the bank does not have much motivation to help you. From the bank's point of view, you need to stay put and sell your house when the market changes. The incentive for a bank to work with you is to avoid foreclosure or ownership of the property. If no potential foreclosure is looming, there is no reason for a bank to help.

Let's say your employer has transferred you. The bank would see this as a potential foreclosure if you move and can't make two mortgage payments. It would be easy to negotiate a short sale under this condition. Typically, the bank would ask you to list the property for 90 days to see if any offers come in. When the real estate agent lists the house, the agent would use the words—possible short sale—in the special section of the listing. When potential homeowners see that, they would assume this is a good deal and would make offers. You would present all offers to the bank reminding them that you have moved and can't make two payments. The bank would take the highest offer and close the deal. The bank does not want the possibility of a foreclosure with a homeowner who has moved out of state.

Let's say you simply want to move and upgrade to a bigger home. If you owe more than your house is worth, the bank has no incentive to help you unload your property. Again, the bank would tell you to stay put and sell the house when the market comes back. Explain to the bank that you are going to move and that you will deed the house back if necessary. Staying put is not an option. If the bank does agree to help, it would ask you to list the house to see what offers come in. In the past, the bank would not even consider this option. Because of two million foreclosures and rising, most banks are offering to help anyone who wants to move. They are concerned about what could happen if they say no. We are seeing banks ask for a 90-day listing, keep all of the offers, wait until the 90 days has expired, and then ask for a "best and highest" offer. Meaning the bank would have the real estate agents contact all the people who made offers asking them to make one final, highest offer.

The bank would set a deadline—say Friday at 5:00 PM. Let's say you have four offers during the 90-day period. Each of these four people would submit one final sealed offer as high as they are willing to go. The offers are sealed to prevent real estate agents from knowing what each person offered so that the agents won't be tempted to tell their client what the highest offer is in order to secure the purchase. The bank opens the sealed bids at 5:00 PM and, if any are in the ballpark, accepts the highest offer with the best terms. If you offered $100,000 *cash* and we offered $105,000 *based on financing,* the bank would take the cash offer. If the cash offer falls through, the bank would have the real estate agent contact the person who had the second highest offer to negotiate price and terms that are acceptable to the bank.

Another common offer banks are making to upside-down sellers is to release the property for a lesser amount and have the homeowners sign an unsecured note for the balance. For example—you owe $200,000 on your house and it is worth $160,000 in this market and you want to sell. You get an offer for $160,000 and call the bank. The bank agrees to allow the sale, but you have to sign a promissory note for the $40,000 dollar shortage. While we don't recommend this, but it is another option. If you want out of your house bad enough, you may be willing to do this. If you buy a new house and sell it in the future for a profit, the promissory note would get paid off. By using this option, you would not have a foreclosure or a short sale or anything on your credit report because you have agreed, in advance, to pay the bank what it might otherwise lose and have signed a note for it. This note is unsecured and could be wiped out in bankruptcy.

Again, if there is no threat of foreclosure and you simply owe more than your house is worth, the bank does not have much incentive to accept less than what you owe so you may be stuck waiting until the market changes and property values begin to rise again.

CHAPTER 5

Try a Loan Modification: Negotiating a Lower Monthly Payment with Your Lender

As we said in an earlier chapter, there are other options to try before you try a short sale, if you want to try to keep your home until the market turns around. Homeowners and investors alike can use these options, which are covered in this and the next few chapters. These options are simple and can be done by you directly. You do not need the help of a real estate agent or an investor.

A **loan modification** means restructuring the loan you currently have, usually to give you lower payments, so you can afford to keep the property. In order for the bank to consider this, you have to prove that you are now capable of making payments on time again. As we mentioned in the Introduction, many people are in trouble because of mortgage payments that reset with a higher interest rate making the new payment out of reach. If this is the case, you will try to keep the same loan in place and negotiate a new, lower interest rate.

There are many benefits to a loan modification. The main one being that the foreclosure is completely stopped and you are starting with a clean slate. With a **forbearance agreement** (which we discuss next) you are still in a pending state of foreclosure while you repay the back payments.

47

Loan Modification

Most of you who are in trouble have already received several letters from the bank offering to work something out. Often homeowners or investors are so embarrassed by their situation that they hide behind their answering machine and will not speak to the bank. Banks are willing to give you a chance to repay the loan, but you don't know that if you are avoiding the bank's calls. Even if you have several investment properties, contact the bank. The banks can be surprisingly easy to work with. It is easier for us to avoid the calls because we don't want to face what is happening. It reflects on our mindset—embarrassment, anger, denial. See how mindset keeps popping up? We are often our own worst enemy.

Contact the bank and ask for one of these:

➤ The Loss Mitigation Department.

➤ The Workout Department.

➤ The Late Payment Department.

➤ The Bankruptcy Department.

Most banks have a workout department; however, it is common to get someone on the phone who has no idea who to transfer you to. In this case, persist in asking that you be transferred to someone else who might be able to help you. Eventually, you will reach someone who should be able to connect you to the right department.

Before you consider a loan modification, consider why you want one. Do you really want to keep your property or are you in denial? Be honest with yourself. If you are in denial, take some time to accept your difficult situation before calling the bank to work something out. It is more difficult to work out an option when you are working off of sheer emotion. The bank is logical while you are emotional. It will be difficult to be open-minded and neutral if your emotions are running high.

If you are still embarrassed, try to work through that as well. It is difficult to talk to a bank representative who does not care about the outcome as much as you do. The bank representative will ask many personal questions and you can't

be too embarrassed to answer them. Now is the time to lay all
your cards on the table and do the best job you possibly can
negotiating one of the options.

Don't even think about calling the bank if you are still
angry. Yelling at bank representatives will only cause them to
hang up on you and may ruin your chances to make a deal. Your
best chance for success is to get on the phone well prepared,
be calm and assertive, and ask for what you want.

Before you attempt a loan modification or a forbearance
agreement, you must be prepared:

- Have your financial records in hand.
- Know your total net income.
- Know your total debt—including emergency funds.
- Know your market—what houses are selling for.
- Have copies of paychecks—if any.
- Have copies of late notices—phone bills, electric, mortgage, car payments, and so on.
- Have copies of credit card statements.
- Have copies of any medical bills, divorce papers, job layoffs, increased mortgage payments, and so on.
- Show proof you evicted nonpaying tenants and that you have vacant rentals.
- Have a repair list ready.
- Have anything handy that you think might be important.

Before the bank will work out a repayment plan, it wants
to make sure you actually have a provable hardship. The more
proof you have, the easier it is to work something out. Whether
a homeowner or an investor, banks are willing to give you a
second chance as long as you can prove how you will make
the new payments.

Based on what you prepared, the bank will decide to accept or reject repayments. If the bank says no, a short sale will
be your next option. If you don't qualify for repayment, the
bank will also realize it and will be more open to accepting a
short sale.

The bank prefers a repayment plan because it will get paid back all the money due. If the bank accepts a short sale, it loses money. Banks are in the business of lending money, not losing money. Likewise, banks are in the business of lending money, not owning property. Given the choice, a bank will do a loan modification or a forbearance agreement in lieu of a short sale.

Trying these options first makes your chances for a short sale much better. The bank representatives have seen for themselves that repayment is not possible, they know that you might file bankruptcy and drag this one on for a very long time, they see the market is still dropping, and they realize that a short sale is a solid option.

Possible Options When Working Out a Loan Modification

Let's say you have a $200,000 property, you owe $200,000, your mortgage payment is $1,500, and you are $15,000 behind in payments. Because you are not making mortgage payments or you are collecting rent without paying the mortgage, you can get your hands on $2,000. You will offer the bank the $2,000 that you have and then you will make arrangements to repay the rest.

We start by asking the bank to accept the $2,000 and put the rest of the late payments on the back of the loan. This option would make your last payment (at the very end of your loan) a balloon payment. Meaning it would be the regular $1,500 payment, plus the $13,000 you still owe due in one large payment. If the bank says no . . . keep asking.

Offer to pay the $2,000 now and modify the loan to create a new loan. If the bank accepts this offer, it could modify your current loan several ways. You may be able to sign new loan papers and start completely over. The bank would take your outstanding mortgage balance, the amount you are behind in payments, attorney's fees, and whatever else it can dream up and give you a new total. Then it would take the new total and have you sign brand new loan papers giving you a chance to start over from scratch.

The downside to this is that if you have already paid on your mortgage for 10 years, you now have a new 30-year loan again. You will pay a lot in interest if you accept this option, but you will be able to keep your property. Also, if the bank gives you a new 30-year loan, it will most likely raise your interest rate. If you were unable to afford the interest payment before it might be even tougher now. Be realistic before doing a loan modification.

What we would prefer to see happen is for the bank to accept the $2,000 down and then take the remaining payments and spread them evenly over the time you have left on your loan. If you have been paying on your mortgage for 10 years, the bank takes the $13,000 and divides it equally over the 20 years remaining. Your interest rate stays the same, your payment increases a very small amount, and you don't pay a new set of closing costs. We prefer this loan modification to the other.

Again, the main benefit to a loan modification is that the loan starts new and the foreclosure is stopped. If a homeowner falls behind on payments again, the bank has to start the foreclosure process over from the beginning.

Sample Conversation with the Bank

You have gathered your paperwork and mustered up the courage to call the bank. Your conversation will go something like this:

You: Hi, my name is_____; my loan number is _____. Can you pull me up on the computer?

Bank: Got it. What can I do for you?

You: As you can see, I am several mortgage payments behind, and I'd like to work out a repayment plan. I have saved _____ (whatever amount of money you can get your hands on) and can apply it to my mortgage and then maybe we can work out the rest.

Bank: I see your back payments are $15,000 and you have _____ to work with. What is it you'd like to do?

You: I heard about a loan modification and I'd like to work out one of those. I understand that **according to my mortgage I am entitled to one a year,** but no more than four during the life of my loan. I am hoping that this one will be the only one I ever need.

Bank: Before I can consider a loan modification, our bank needs to see that you are capable of making on-time payments again. What has changed in your situation?

You: **Explain**—you are working again, you could afford the payment before the loan reset, you rented out your investment properties, you took on a roommate, or whatever has happened.

Bank: This sounds good. Can you send some proof of the hardship as well as how you are going to start making on-time payments again? Maybe paycheck stubs, rental agreements, bank statements, or whatever you can provide showing that you can make the new payments. Also, I need proof of hardship in order to get my boss's approval (send cut-off notices, late payments, letters from the bank, whatever you have that proves extreme hardship).

It's that easy. The bank will do all the paperwork so that all you have to do is get the papers signed and get a fresh start. If you are unable to prove that you can make new, higher payments, the bank will most likely say no to a loan modification. The bank knows that if it accepts a loan modification, it has to start from scratch in order to take the property in foreclosure.

Typically, if the bank is not certain it will get paid, the bank agrees to work out a forbearance agreement instead.

Forbearance Agreement

A forbearance agreement is a repayment plan as well (see Figure 5.1). The main difference being that this is a short term agreement and that the outstanding balance is added to your regular payment often increasing your payment by hundreds of dollars each month.

FIGURE 5.1   Sample Forbearance Agreement (Downloadable*)

This agreement is between _____ (homeowners) and _____ (bank) and is an agreement for repayment of delinquent payments.

_____ (homeowners) current mortgage payment is $1,500 and is due on the first day of each month. _____ (homeowners) are currently $15,000 behind in mortgage payments. _____ (bank) and _____ (homeowners) have agreed to the following:

$2,000 is due immediately and the balance of $13,000 will be paid over 24 months in equal payments. This following is the agreed upon repayment for the next 24 months:

Due Date	Current Payment ($)	Delinquent Amount ($)	Total Due ($)
Jan 1	1,500	542	2,042
Feb 1	1,500	542	2,042
March 1	1,500	542	2,042
April 1	1,500	542	2,042
May 1	1,500	542	2,042
June 1	1,500	542	2,042
July 1	1,500	542	2,042
Aug 1	1,500	542	2,042
Sept 1	1,500	542	2,042
Oct 1	1,500	542	2,042
Nov 1	1,500	542	2,042
Dec 1	1,500	542	2,042
Jan 1	1,500	542	2,042
Feb 1	1,500	542	2,042
March 1	1,500	542	2,042
April 1	1,500	542	2,042
May 1	1,500	542	2,042
June 1	1,500	542	2,042

(continued)

FIGURE 5.1   (Continued)

July 1	1,500	542	2,042
Aug 1	1,500	542	2,042
Sept 1	1,500	542	2,042
Oct 1	1,500	542	2,042
Nov 1	1,500	542	2,042
Dec 1	1,500	542	2,042

Payments must be received in our office _____ (address of the bank) on or before the 1st of each month in the form of a cashier's check made payable to the bank.

_____ (homeowners) agree that any missed payments will void this forbearance agreement and the bank will resume the pending foreclosure. Homeowners also understand that they are still in foreclosure during this entire agreement and that when the final payment is received the pending foreclosure will be stopped.

_____   _____

Homeowner   Date

_____   _____

Bank   Date

Let's use the same example as previously. You have a property worth $200,000. The property is worth $200,000, the mortgage payments are the same as above—$1,500 and you are $15,000 behind. Assume you have saved $2,000 dollars.

You contact the bank and give them the same basic script. After reviewing your information, the bank decides a forbearance agreement is the best option for the bank. The bank accepts the $2,000 and then takes the $13,000 you still owe and divides it into 24 equal payments, which is $542 a month. The $542 is **added** to your original payment of $1,500 increasing your payment to $2,042 a month for the next 24 months!

If you had a difficult time affording $1,500, how can you afford $2,042? Twenty-four months is a long time to have such a high payment. If this is a rental property, will rent cover the new payment? If you are not sure, don't do a forbearance agreement.

The upside to a forbearance agreement is that it buys you time to sell the house or try to solve your problem. The downside is that you are in a "pending" state of foreclosure the entire 24 months. If you were 30 days from the foreclosure sale date, you will stay 30 days from the foreclosure sale date for the entire 24 months. What the bank does is postpone the sale date each month. If you miss a payment, the bank sells the house the next month.

Should you stop making the payments, you can call the bank and ask for another forbearance agreement as long as you can come up with another down payment. If you just used all the money you had for the last down payment, it might be more difficult to come up with money again.

As you can see, the forbearance agreement is simple. It typically includes the delinquent amount, the new payment, the dates the payment is due, and a signature. The bank will prepare this agreement for you. If you choose this option, please make your payments on time.

CHAPTER 6

Government Programs and Mortgage Relief Organizations

To get help from the government, you'll need to spend a lot of time trying to navigate the bureaucracy, but it can be worth it. One place to start is in the white pages or on the Internet. There are many agencies that offer emergency payments for electric bills, water, mortgage payments (more difficult on an investment property), food, diapers, baby milk, insurance, doctors, and much, much more.

The downside to using a government organization is that the red tape can take so long. If you need emergency assistance, you might not have 30 days to wait.

Most cities have local government funding. These departments are given a budget each year and if they don't use the entire budget, they lose it or it is reduced.

There are also grants for home repairs—handy for investors—down payments on another property, closing costs grants, and many more. With most grants, you have to live in the property for at least two years and then the money is yours without repayment. If you move or sell before then, you have to pay the money back.

We have a very good friend, Chris Johnson, who specializes in free government money. Chris generously provided a list of these sites for you. For more information, contact him at www.ChrisFreeMoneyJohnson.com—he is happy to help in any way possible.

Start with mortgage relief sites first. If you are struggling with your mortgage payments, these sites will have a faster reaction time. Trying to get actual cash from the government is much more difficult than getting help with your mortgage payments. We have listed these sites in order of who is easier and quicker to work with. If you choose to contact the agencies, contact them all at once. Do not make the mistake of waiting on a return call from one before calling the next. Remember, these are government agencies and are bogged down because of the mortgage crisis.

If you don't hear back from these agencies in a few days, contact them again. We prefer to call on the phone as opposed to e-mailing. It is too easy for e-mail to get lost in the shuffle, end up in spam, and so on. Personal contact is always better. The person answering the phone might be overwhelmed by the intensity of their job so be patient. You need to build good rapport to get faster results.

Explain that you are behind on your mortgage payments and need their help. Ask what they need from you and get it to them as quickly as possible. Just as you would when negotiating a loan modification or a forbearance agreement, have your paperwork handy. You will have to show proof of hardship. The agency will either send you the necessary papers or send you to a web site to download them. Fill the papers out as quickly as possible and get the ball rolling. Many of these agencies respond very quickly.

Mortgage Relief

HomeFree-USA "Save A Family" Foreclosure Prevention Fund

www.homefreeusa.org/ht/d/sp/i/4943/pid/4943/

Thousands of American families face threats to their homeownership every day. Unemployment, illness, and predatory lending practices threaten the most valuable investment that a homeowner can possess—their home. On average, five families call HomeFree-USA for help every day. As a HUD approved housing counseling agency, HomeFree-USA is required to help these at-risk families with no charge to them.

In some cases, they need help to pay the mortgage for a month or two. In other cases, they need an advocate and assistance with their lender to forestall foreclosure. In all instances, a significant amount of time and/or money must be spent to ensure a positive outcome.

With more than a decade of experience and a 0 percent foreclosure rate, HomeFree-USA has the knowledge, experience, and willingness to help at-risk families successfully protect their homes.

To help with the financial aspects of saving a family, HomeFree-USA has established the "Save a Family" foreclosure prevention fund. HomeFree-USA solicits contributions to this fund to offset expenses related to saving a family from the pain and degradation caused by the loss of a home. These expenses may include funding to ensure that at-risk families have basic necessities such as goods and clothing as well as housing.

Hope Now Alliance

www.hopenow.com/members/members.html

The Hope Now Alliance is a cooperative effort between the U.S. government, counselors, investors, and lenders to help homeowners who may not be able to pay their mortgages. Created in response to the subprime mortgage crisis, the alliance claims to have helped over one million homeowners avoid foreclosure.

Home Equity Loss Prevention Program (HELP)

www.acornhousing.org/TEXT/fap8.php

If you are behind on your mortgage, ACORN housing counselors may be able to intervene on your behalf with your lender in order to come to a resolution that will ultimately bring your loan current. The HELP program has established relationships with 43 major lenders in the United States in order to get loans out of foreclosure. Recently, they assisted over 4,800 families in working out repayment plans, forbearance plans, loan modifications, refinances, and partial claims, which allowed these families to keep the equity that they built in their homes.

Mortgage Relief Fund

www.mortgagerelieffund.com

The Mortgage Relief initiative has grown from five regional banks to nearly 50 banks of every size, with branches throughout much of New England. The participating banks represent a safe and sound place to discuss your credit needs and financial situation, with expertise and respect.

Whenever possible, the banks participating in the initiative will help eligible homeowners refinance into conventional loans that will better meet their needs. The banks aim to help homeowners who are having difficulty making payments (or expect to) because of high-rate, nontraditional, or resetting loans.

Housing Partnership Fund

www.housingpartnership.net/lending/housing_partnership _fund/

The Housing Partnership Fund is a CDFI-certified lending affiliate of the Housing Partnership Network that provides members with short-term, equity-like financing for affordable housing rental and ownership development.

The Fund's loans, which offer terms of up to three years, generally bridge public subsidies that are not committed at the time of acquisition.

Veterans' Mortgage Relief

www1.va.gov/opa/pressrel/pressrelease.cfm?id=1514/

Many homeowners have found it difficult recently to pay their mortgages, but quick intervention by loan counselors at the Department of Veterans Affairs (VA) has actually reduced the number of veterans defaulting on their home loans.

Depending on a veteran's circumstances, the VA can intercede with the borrower on the veteran's behalf to pursue options—such as repayment plans, forbearance, and loan modifications—that would allow a veteran to keep a home.

With the aid of many of these agencies, you may be able to keep your home or work out some type of repayment plan with your bank. Spend a few hours this week and surf the Web to see if any of these might work for you. As we mentioned earlier, if these agencies do not use their budgets, they lose them. They are just as motivated as you are.

Financial Relief

Soldiers' and Sailors' Civil Relief Act

www.defenselink.mil/specials/Relief_Act_Revision/

If you are a reserve component service member called to active duty, you may qualify for any or all of the following:

➤ Reduced interest rate on mortgage payments.
➤ Reduced interest rate on credit card debt.
➤ Protection from eviction if your rent is $1,200 or less.
➤ Delay of all civil court actions, such as bankruptcy, foreclosure, or divorce proceedings.

Housing Choice Tenant-Based Voucher

www.hud.gov/offices/pih/programs/hcv/tenant.cfm

This program enables a family to choose housing, then rental subsidy payments are made to the owner to subsidize occupancy by the family.

Low Income Home Energy Assistance Program
http://liheap.ncat.org/sp.htm

LIHEAP offers one-time financial assistance to qualifying low-income households who require support in paying their home heating or cooling bills.

PART II

Short Sales: How to Sell a House When It's Worth Less Than You Owe

CHAPTER 7

The Short Sale Solution

Y ou've tried a loan modification and a forbearance agreement, and you've tried to get help from a local government agency. Nothing has worked and now you realize that you must sell your house even though the mortgage is more than the value of the house. It's time to contact the "loss mitigation" department of your bank and get to work.

Remember what we said earlier, selling your house is not the end of the world. Whether an investor or a homeowner, life will get better now. Once you begin the short sale process, you are almost home free. You get the short sale accepted, you get the house sold, you get moved into an apartment, and you begin sleeping again. Life starts to get easy and fun again.

Please don't dwell on the past. One of the biggest mistakes you could make is to beat yourself up over what is happening to you. There is nothing you can do to undo the past. What you can do is move forward with a happy heart. Every single person reading this book has made mistakes, done something they wish they hadn't, or said something they wish they could take back. It's what makes us human. Trust us when we tell you, we have both made some bonehead decisions in our past. Every now and then, we still do something that doesn't work out the way we thought it would and we wonder what the heck we were thinking. The good news is that we laugh, forgive ourselves, and move on. God says to forgive others as *you* would like to be forgiven. That means total forgiveness for whatever someone has done to wrong you.

Maybe during this difficult time, people have turned their backs on you. Don't dwell on it. Forgive the people and move on. It is important to your sanity. This book is written to help you get a fresh start—this means in every area of your life.

Again, a short sale is when you negotiate with a bank to accept less than what is owed against your property. For example, you have a property worth $125,000 and you owe $125,000. Your mortgage payment reset and you can't afford the new payments. To top it off, you are getting divorced. Life seems hopeless. You read this book, follow what it says, and contact your bank to work out a short sale. After some strategic steps, the bank says yes. You get the bank to agree to accept $75,000 as full payment and now you are able to sell your house and start fresh.

If you are able to get a short sale accepted, you can use the methods we discussed in Chapter 2 to try to sell your property. The easiest, fastest way to sell your house will be to sell it to an investor. If you are an investor who is upside down, you'd be surprised how other investors will step up to help. Of course, they are going to want a great deal, especially in this market.

In the past, banks would only consider a short sale when the payments were late. With all of the interest-only loans and with payments resetting at record speed, banks are accepting short sales on properties that are not yet late. If you can prove that you have no more money to continue making payments, the bank will open a short sale file.

If it is an investment property, the bank will still open a file. With over two million short sales, banks are worried about going under. The government can only step in and help so much. Eventually, banks will go broke if foreclosures keep increasing. Many bank stocks have dropped dramatically in the past year. These are all good tips to know when negotiating a short sale.

This new government bailout is going to bail out the banks, but WE must bail out the homeowners. Banks will be freed of the properties they currently own, but this has no bearing on the people who are facing financial hardship. Unless every loan in America is reset back to the original low payment that was affordable, foreclosures will continue to rise.

In the past, homeowners could not negotiate their own short sales. Banks did not want to negotiate with a homeowner directly. Banks wanted either an investor or a real estate agent. Currently, homeowners, investors, real estate agents, anyone can call the bank and start a short sale file. The key to short sale success is to have a good package put together and to sound as if you know what you are doing. Remember, no one knows this is your very first attempt at a short sale except you. Even as a homeowner, you can sound confident.

Creating a good package is crucial to your short sale success. You'll need things like area comparable sales, a hardship letter, proof of hardship, a list of repairs and things like that. We are going to talk more about the details of a short sale soon and we'll give you what you need for each step along the way.

Bottom line, a short sale is one of your best options for getting free of your underwater property and moving on with your life.

When a Short Sale Won't Work

There is no real instance when a short sale won't work. Banks will consider a short sale on every foreclosure whether it is a residential property, commercial, mobile home, condo, investment property, or anything else. The goal of the loss mitigation department is to mitigate losses, that is, working out a short sale:

- ➤ If you make no effort to show the benefits to the bank, you might get a no.
- ➤ If you can't prove hardship, you might get a no.
- ➤ If you are too emotional and can't deal with the bank representative in a professional and calm manner, you might get a no. If this is the case, work with an investor.
- ➤ If the bank representative is swamped with too many deals and can't make time for your deal before the sale date, you might get a no.
- ➤ If you are calling the bank too close to the sheriff's sale, you might get a no.

There are many reasons you might get a no, but there are just as many reasons why you might get a yes:

> ➤ The bank has too many foreclosures and needs to get them off the books.
> ➤ It's the end of the quarter, quarterly reports are due that go to shareholders, and the bank needs to clean up the books.
> ➤ It's the end of the year, the year-end reports are due, and the bank needs to clean up the books.
> ➤ You built a really good hardship case and made the numbers make sense to the bank.
> ➤ The bank has too many defaulted loans on the books right now and needs to get rid of as many as possible.

When preparing your short sale, look at it as if you are an attorney going to court to win a case. The more information you provide and the more research you do, the more likely you are to win. Attorneys don't win cases just by showing up, they prepare. This is the same mentality you must have when working a short sale. The more preparation, the less likely to get a no.

Short Sale Requirements

As we discussed, banks do short sales for many reasons—too many properties in default, quarterly reports due, year-end reports due, you built a good case, they are worried that you might file bankruptcy and stall the process, you have several properties and the bank wants to cut its losses, and many more reasons.

What the bank requires is lots of real information to prove your case. Gather as much information as you possibly can. Start working on your list today. The items in the following list are not required by the bank, but they will help you get a yes. The bank doesn't usually have a specific requirement other than proof of an actual hardship. It is very easy to prove hardship because it is real. Start today and gather some items that will help you with your short sale:

- ➤ A cover letter stating why you are asking for the short sale. Depending on your status, use different cover letters here—one from a homeowner's point of view (Figure 7.1) and a different one from an investor's point of view.
- ➤ A hardship letter describing your situation with as much detail as possible and lots of proof—investors and homeowners alike need to do this step.
- ➤ Low comparable sales or other foreclosures or distressed properties in your area.
- ➤ Pictures of any areas that require repair that your property might have.
- ➤ A net sheet showing the bank what it will make, after expenses, if it accepts the short sale. The title company doing the closing will do this for you.
- ➤ A sales contract showing that you have a buyer—if you don't have a buyer yet, now is a good time to start looking for one.
- ➤ Some statistics showing how many properties are on the market right now compared to last year.
- ➤ Have a real estate agent prepare a list of price drops in the last three months.
- ➤ A list of the registered sex offenders in your area—this is not necessary, but has a great shock value when trying to negotiate with an out-of-state bank.
- ➤ Pictures of boarded up houses in the area.
- ➤ Pictures of new construction in the area.
- ➤ Crime reports in the county and neighborhood.
- ➤ Tax returns showing your loss of income.
- ➤ Copies of medical bills.
- ➤ Copies of any and all late bills and payments—phone, electric, credit cards, water, car payments, insurance, or anything else that you can get your hands on.

FIGURE 7.1   Homeowner Hardship Letter (Downloadable*)

Dear Mr. Banker:

I am writing this letter to share some of the hardships I have endured over the past year. As you know, my property located at 8172 Smith Street is currently facing foreclosure. **I have tried to sell the property for months and have gotten only one serious offer because of the poor condition of the property.** Based on the offer I have, I urge you to please accept the $140,000 offer being submitted by Bill and Dwan.

Please accept this offer as payment in full. **My attorney has advised me to file bankruptcy, but I prefer to avoid further destruction of my credit.** I just want to move on and start over. I am so burned out and don't want to fight anymore.

I am enclosing my bank statements from the past several months; late notices on my car, credit cards, mortgage payments, utilities, and anything else I can find that shows the financial trouble I'm facing. I have also enclosed my last year's tax returns.

I was laid off several months ago and have been unable to find a new job. I can't sleep, I am stressed out, my wife/husband and I are fighting, my kids are emotional wrecks because we have to move, we have no family to help us, and we are at the end of our rope. You are the only hope we have. You are the only person who can give us a fresh start. We are really counting on your bank to give us a clean break.

If there is any other information you need, please feel free to call me.

Sincerely,

Distressed Homeowner

*Copyright © 2009 by Dwan-Bent Twyford and Bill Twyford. To download and customize this form for your personal use, please visit www.theieu.com/underwaterform.

- ➤ Paycheck stubs.
- ➤ Bank statements showing that you have no money.
- ➤ If you have any accounts that got closed, send that as well.
- ➤ If you have pawned anything to pay bills or for groceries, show the stub for that.
- ➤ If you have filed bankruptcy—show the papers.
- ➤ If you are going through a divorce, show the lawyer's papers and fees.
- ➤ If you are involved in a probate situation, show whatever paperwork you have.
- ➤ Anything else you can think of that will show the bank all the reasons it should accept a discount and let the property go for less so that you can get a fresh start in life.

The more information you can provide, the more hardship you can prove, *and* the nicer you are to the bank representative, the better your chances will be to get a deeper discount. The deeper the discount, the easier it will be for you to sell the property and get a fresh start.

Short Sales for Investment Properties

In the past, banks weren't as excited to work with investors losing properties as much as they are today. The banks figured it was an investment property, not a primary residence, and there was no reason to short sale it. With bankruptcies at an all-time high, banks are more inclined to work with investors. If the properties were bought in the name of a legal entity—corporation, LLC, and so on—the investor can file Chapter 11 and liquidate assets. Chapter 7 and 13 are for personal use. Investors know how to work the bankruptcy process as well as homeowners do. Banks are painfully aware of this.

When putting together the short sale package for investment properties, send the same items a homeowner would send. The only difference would be to write a different type of hardship letter, something like Figure 7.2.

FIGURE 7.2   Investor Hardship Letter (Downloadable*)

Dear Loss Mitigation,

I am writing to explain the hardships I have been facing in recent months. I bought four properties several years ago to keep as rentals. My plan was to rent them, pay the mortgages off, and use them to subsidize my retirement. Unfortunately, with the housing crisis, rents have fallen in this area. I now have four rentals that I can't collect enough rent from to cover the mortgage payments. I have no personal money to subsidize the monthly shortages. I have borrowed money from four different banks, so I am contacting each of you to ask for help.

I am now three payments behind and facing foreclosure on each of my rentals. I would like to sell these properties instead of losing them in a foreclosure. I have spoken to several other investors in town who have agreed to buy one or more of them, but not for what I owe. I am asking you to please accept _____ as payment in full for my property.

I understand that your bank does short sales. I have prepared some financial information as proof that I am in trouble. Even though these are not my primary residence, please consider the short sale. I am losing everything; I can't sleep at night; my spouse and I are fighting; I am considering bankruptcy to get a fresh start. My attorney says I can file a Chapter 7 for my personal residence and a Chapter 11 for my business. The thought of this makes me feel ill, but I have to do something. I am at my wits end and need help. Because of the loss of rents, I can't keep up with the taxes or insurance. I just pray that no one gets hurt on my property.

Please look over the enclosed information and consider my offer. The person willing to buy these properties from me can close in two weeks.

Sincerely,

Investor in Distress

As you can see, this letter is not that different from what a homeowner would write. The point is to show the bank why you can't afford the property. Banks will short sale investment properties as well as residential. We did a short sale of a commercial building from $300,000 to $137,000 and paid cash. The property is now worth $800,000 and paid for. You can short sale anything.

How to Approach Your Bank

When negotiating a short sale, it is important to understand the mindset of loss mitigation. We spoke of the different mindsets and emotions you might be experiencing. The bank has different mindsets.

Currently, the average loss mitigation representative has well over 500 files on any given day. Think about that—500 files! They are overworked and underpaid. The average loss mitigation representative only lasts seven months on the job. It's a tough department of the bank to work in. All day long you work with people losing houses and people yelling at you.

Knowing that the representative you are assigned to is swamped will help you better negotiate. Have your paperwork ready, be willing to negotiate, be ready to talk openly about your situation, don't get argumentative, understand the representative's position. Since most loss mitigation representatives are accustomed to working with investors, it is difficult for them to talk directly with homeowners because they aren't sure what they can say without hurting your feelings. Let the representative know that all topics are open for discussion and that you won't be hurt or embarrassed to talk about your distress.

The typical loss mitigation representative lives in another state. Say you are in Texas, the loss mitigation representative may live in California. The representative will most likely be where the bank has its regional headquarters—usually Texas, California, Utah, or Florida. Bank representatives are trying to make a decision about your property based on property values where they live. If you have a bank representative living in California and you live in Alabama, they may not understand why properties are so cheap and why you need a short sale in the first place. Likewise, if you live in California and the bank representative is in Texas, it is difficult to understand why properties are so expensive.

Because of the difference in property values nationwide, the bank will send a licensed real estate agent to the house to give the bank a neutral opinion of value or brokers price opinion (BPO). Let's say the bank representative is in California and your property is located in Iowa. All major banks have local real estate offices they work with to sell the properties after the properties have gone to the sheriff's sale. In this case, let's say the bank works with ReMax. The loss mitigation representative will call a local Iowa ReMax office and ask for a BPO.

A local real estate agent will go to the property, take some pictures, run some local comparable sales, and then report the findings to the bank representative in California. The bank representative in California will then take that opinion into consideration when you are asking for a short sale. If you have a house worth $200,000 and you owe $200,000 and the real estate agent tells the bank it is also worth $200,000, it is more difficult to get a deep short sale. If the real estate agent tells the bank representative it is worth $125,000, the bank is more likely to give you a deeper discount.

Whether a homeowner or an investor, the key to a successful short sale is a good BPO. When we are helping a homeowner in distress, we always meet the person doing the BPO in person at the property. We tell the bank that the homeowners don't want to deal with the stress and that we will meet the agent at the house to show the property. If you are the homeowner in distress doing your own short sale, it is crucial to meet the agent at the house and show them around.

This can be a difficult step for you because you have to point out all the negative things about your property, talk about your situation, and more. By approaching the bank in a humble spirit and scheduling the BPO as soon as possible, you will find the bank far more willing to work with you.

How to Ace the Broker's Price Opinion

Whether an investor or a homeowner, it is important to do the BPO in person. It is also important to understand that the person doing the BPO is only getting paid about $75 or so. Many times the agents doing the BPOs will do what is called a "drive-by" meaning they will simply drive by the property, take a picture from the road, and not even see the inside of the property. We understand that they do that because they feel it is not worth their time, but how can you give a true opinion of value without seeing the inside of the property?

Again, whether an investor or a homeowner, the goal is the same . . . to make the person doing the BPO see the property from *your* point of view. In order for that to happen, you have to build a case with the agent just like you have to build a case with the loss mitigation representative. Many investors don't think that this step is that big of a deal, but we are here to tell you—it is. You must try to meet the agent in person. If it is absolutely not possible to meet face-to-face then speak to the agent on the phone and do a BPO verbally. However you do it, the key is that it *must* be done.

Here are our best tips to a successful BPO:

➤ Show the agent around the house and point out every detail of anything that might need repair.
➤ Explain your situation—in detail. If you are an investor, tell the homeowners story for them.
➤ Tell the agent exactly what amount you offered the bank.
➤ Give the agent copies of pictures of disrepair.
➤ Give the agent copies of the low comparable sales that you ran or had an agent run for you (Figure 7.3).
➤ If you have children, show the agent the kid's rooms and explain how difficult this has been for you and the kids.
➤ Tell the agent that without his or her help, that you and your family will be homeless and that you can't do this without a low opinion of value.

➢ Talk to the agent about crime in the county, sex offenders, low sales, markets dropping, and other things along those lines.

➢ Explain that you can't sleep, you are stressed out, you simply want a chance to get a fresh start, and they are the person who can help you start over.

➢ It doesn't hurt if you don't clean for a few days or carry out the trash.

➢ If your property does have a lot of disrepair—don't fix anything before the BPO. We have had homeowners clean and repair things because they knew the real estate agent would be in their house and the homeowners didn't want the agent to see that the house was a mess...it was and we wanted to show that. It hurt their BPO. We now ask people to leave things be until the agent has come.

➢ If you can muster up a tear, it certainly won't hurt.

The point is to get the BPO agent to go back to the bank with the lowest opinion of value as possible. Showing disrepair, talking about your tough situation, and speaking of area problems most definitely influence the agent's opinion. Most agents who do BPOs think like a homeowner, not an investor. A typical homeowner would see a house that needs paint and carpet and think it is a disaster, while a typical investor would see the same thing and think it is a fixer-upper with major potential. If you are a homeowner, you must try to think like an investor during the BPO and separate your emotions from the property. We know that this is easier said than done, but you must try.

We mentioned that a tear would not hurt. When we say to separate your emotions we mean for you to show the house in the worst possible light and really be open-minded about what your house needs. Often people have lived with disrepair for so long that they no longer see it. We have been in houses that were trashed and the homeowners didn't see what we saw that needed repair. If you are not sure of the real condition of your house ask a friend or family member or hire a home inspector to give you a list of repairs. Home inspectors can be found in the Yellow Pages, but they do charge for their services. Friends

FIGURE 7.3   Agent Letter (Downloadable*)

Dear Loss Mitigation Rep,

My name is Sally Johnson, and I am a real estate agent for XYZ Agency. I have reviewed the property located at 1825 Smith Street. I understand that the property is in foreclosure and that the homeowners are trying to do a short sale. The owners ask me for an opinion of value.

I did some research and have enclosed two comparable sales. There are many more to back these up:

354 Smith Street	$85,000
777 Elm Street	$91,000

During a short sale, I understand that banks typically send an agent to give an opinion of value. I work this area and am certain of the value. I ask you to consider the short sale because this property will not move quickly.

I am happy to provide a listing agreement if your bank requires one. Please call if I can be of service to you.

Sincerely,

Sally Johnson

XYZ Realty

*Copyright © 2009 by Dwan-Bent Twyford and Bill Twyford. To download and customize this form for your personal use, please visit www.theieu.com/underwaterform.

and family members are your best bet as long as you won't be mad at what they say or hold it against them. If they think you might take it personally, they most likely won't give you an honest opinion because they want to maintain their relationship with you.

Bottom line—the BPO is crucial to your short sale. It is much easier to get a bank representative to drop 40 percent or 50 percent of the property value if the BPO comes in low. If there was no effort put into the BPO, the agent will give a high opinion—thinking that is what everyone wants. Typically, an agent is asked to give a high opinion of value because homeowners are trying to sell a property and want a high value to get as much money as possible. Remember: If you don't tell them what you want, you won't get it.

If your property has an FHA or VA loan, the bank will send an appraiser instead of a real estate agent. Because those loans are government guaranteed, they must be appraised by an FHA/VA approved appraiser. You will do the exact same thing with an appraiser as you would with a real estate agent—do a great walk through, show the house from your point of view, give pictures, talk about the hard times, and so on.

When a house is appraised, appraisers have a low range and a high range in which to work. All we are asking for is the lowest range possible. For example, houses in your area might sell anywhere from $125 to $200 a square foot. If the appraiser gives us a value in the $125 or less range, we would most likely get a better short sale. If the appraiser came in at the $200 or more price range, we might have a harder time getting the bank to come way down on price.

We do want to issue a word of warning: If for some reason there is no possible way to attend the BPO or do one on the phone, please move forward with the short sale. The fact that you are in distress or possibly in foreclosure is reason enough for the bank to consider the short sale. The short sale is given because of some type of distress. A low BPO can help to get a deeper discount—it does not kill the deal.

To watch an actual BPO, go to www.youtube.com/dwanbentwyford and watch a live BPO. You will find it very educational and funny.

CHAPTER 8

How to Put Together Your Own Short Sale Package

To make this chapter easier to understand, we are going to explain how to do your own short sale package and then at the end of the chapter we will include a sample package. Once you see it all laid out, you will see just how easy it is to do short sales for yourself.

We started doing short sales back in the mid-1990s. Back then, the bank would not even speak to you if you were a homeowner or an investor. We had to tell banks we were friends trying to help. It was true because as an investor in preforeclosure properties, we developed a friendship with every person we ever helped.

As the early 2000s rolled around, banks began working with investors. Foreclosures were climbing and banks didn't want to work with a nonprofessional. If you were a friend or family member, the banks didn't want to speak to you. If you were an investor or real estate agent, the door was wide open. In fact, the banks preferred to work with investors because they knew how to do short sales. The typical loss mitigation representative was accumulating hundreds of files and didn't have time to train newbies. This is one of the reasons we have been so successful teaching short sales. Our students put together great packages, the banks love the packages, and our students are some of the most successful in the country. When we were asked to write this book, we were thrilled to be able to teach homeowners what investors have known for years.

As foreclosures have skyrocketed, banks have begun to work directly with homeowners. This is something we hoped would eventually happen. If you are a seller who is underwater, you can finally help yourself. It is empowering to be able to help yourself and not have to rely on someone else. We are going to teach you how to find an ethical investor in case you get a bank that does not want to work directly with you, but you shouldn't have any problems.

Even more exciting is that banks have started doing short sales even if you are not in foreclosure. If you can prove that you can't make any more payments or that your payments are getting ready to adjust to an amount that is not possible to pay, or that all your rentals are empty and you are on the verge of losing them, many banks will open a short sale file. It is important to know why banks do short sales in order for you to understand why it would open a file:

- ➤ Banks do not want to own property.
- ➤ Banks want to lend money.
- ➤ Banks have quarterly reports due that show how many good loans and how many bad loans it has given.
- ➤ Banks don't want to risk that you will file foreclosure and live free for two years.
- ➤ Banks worry that distressed sellers will trash the house on their way out.
- ➤ Banks worry about vandalism in vacant houses.
- ➤ Banks worry about natural disasters while the house is vacant.

There are many other reasons banks do short sales, but the bottom line is money. When we show you how to present your package, we'll show you how to build some emotion into the deal to get the bank representative on your side.

Requirements for Financially Distressed Homeowners

If you are at least one payment late, we'll consider you under "financially distressed homeowners." In the next section, we talk about what to do if you haven't missed any payments yet.

The number one item the bank requires is proof that your story is true. Anyone can call and state that they can't afford their house anymore and that they want to walk away from it. With proof, banks can be surprisingly easy to work with. Here are the cold, hard facts that the banks have to consider:

➤ Markets are down.

➤ It is taking months to sell properties.

➤ Property values have dropped over 30 percent in most states.

➤ Insurance rates are rising.

➤ Taxes are going up.

➤ Gas is out of control.

➤ Interest rates are up.

➤ Payments are resetting at record increases.

➤ Unemployment is high.

➤ Bankruptcies have never been higher in our country's history.

Banks are painfully aware that these circumstances can lead to increased foreclosures.

If you are behind in payments, but not yet in foreclosure, a short sale is definitely possible. You'll start by contacting the **work-out** department. Your property would not yet be in the loss mitigation department. Typically, loss mitigation comes into the picture once the foreclosure paperwork has been filed. People are often confused about what a foreclosure is and what a preforeclosure is. Here is how we define these terms:

> A **preforeclosure** is a property where the payments are late, but the foreclosure papers have not been filed.

> A **foreclosure** is a property where the foreclosure papers have been filed, but the homeowners still own the house.

> A **bank-owned** property is where the payments were late, the foreclosure papers were filed, the house went to the sheriff's sale, and the bank now owns the property.

Many people consider a foreclosure a property that already went through the entire process and is now owned by the bank. We want to make sure you use the proper terminology so that when you are reading the papers, watching the news, or talking to loss mitigation, you know what everyone is really talking about.

Because financial hardship typically does not happen overnight, gather information from the past two years. Typically, a homeowner begins by missing a payment here and there: being 30 days late on a mortgage payment, missing an insurance payment, being late on a credit card, paying two months of electric at once, and so on. Once the foreclosure is filed, things seem to spin out of control. This is why we want you to gather information from the past two years. It shows the unraveling of your finances.

If you are an investor and bought properties at the top of the market, find articles that show the beginning of the market decline, when your tenants moved out, copies of late payments, and all of the other items we mentioned previously.

Since you are financially distressed, again, proof is your best bet. Start putting your "Proof of Hardship Package" together immediately. Here is a list of information you will need. Gather and photo copy as many of these items as possible:

> Two years of tax returns that show your income has dropped.

> Copies of lay-off notices or proof that you were let go.

> Copies of late electric bills.

➤ If you are involved in a divorce, provide proof.

➤ Copy any medical bills you have had in the past two years.

➤ Articles of real estate market declines in your area.

➤ Copies of the deeds of any investment properties you bought that have dropped in value.

➤ Proof of empty rentals.

➤ Proof of any rentals that were trashed by tenants.

➤ If you are not getting child support, show proof.

➤ Write a letter explaining your hardship—a sample letter is shown in Figure 7.1 (p. 70).

➤ If you or anyone in your family has been to counseling, show proof. Counseling shows emotional distress.

➤ If there is a probate situation, get a copy of the death certificate.

➤ Copies of your bank statements—savings and checking. We are assuming that your cash flow is very low right now. If the bank sees that you have cash, it will want it.

➤ If you have tapped into your 401 or any retirement fund, show that as well. We are going to talk about this later—not going broke over a property.

➤ If you have cashed out a life insurance policy to make mortgage payments, show proof.

➤ Maybe you have used your children's college fund to keep up with the mortgage payments.

➤ If you have pawned something, show proof.

➤ If you are in jail or know the owner of any property who is in jail, that is a definite hardship.

➤ If you have refinanced any property and used the money to make mortgage payments, show proof.

We're sure you get the idea. The more financial hardship you can prove, the deeper the short sale. The deeper the short sale, the easier it will be for you to sell the property and start over.

Something to remember—whether investor or home-owner—whether in distress or not—once a bank accepts a short sale, *you must sell the property*. The bank wants the property off the books.

Requirements for Solvent Homeowners

➤ If you are in a position where your payments are not yet late, but you know you are on the verge of that happening, contact the bank immediately. The bank will want to know why it should consider the short sale. You will have to prove eminent hardship. Write a letter explaining the hardship you are under and back it up with proof, such as:

➤ Proof that your payment is or has reset to a higher amount.

➤ Proof that you can't make the higher payment—use the financial form provided in Figure 8.1.

➤ Bank statements showing that you are about out of money.

➤ Proof that your properties are vacant.

Based on your situation, you may want to ask for an interest rate reduction first. You may have taken a loan that started with a lower interest rate and now the rate has reset to a higher rate making your payment unaffordable. Banks are bending over backward to reduce interest rates in lieu of foreclosure.

If you have rental properties with mortgage payments that are still on time, showing potential hardship might be enough for the bank to accept your short sale. Proof that your properties are vacant should be enough.

Simply contact the "workout department" at your bank and explain that you need to lower your interest rate or you are in risk of going into foreclosure. The bank will send you some papers to fill out that will show why it should lower the rate. The papers are "financial hardship papers." The banks financial hardship paperwork is not the same hardship letter that we want you to write. We want you to bring emotion into the deal. The bank is looking to see if you have cash and just don't want to pay or if you really are facing hardship. If you have plenty of cash, a good job, and just don't want to own the house anymore, you might find a short sale hard to come by.

If a lower interest rate does not solve the problem, ask the bank to consider a short sale. Typically, a bank wants to see that you are behind on payments before it will consider a short sale. In the past few months, banks have been doing short sales with homeowners who are not late. This new trend is due to that fact that banks are buried in foreclosures right now. Anything the bank can do to avoid more foreclosures is great.

In the next section, we will explain the hardship package and then the actual package will follow the explanations. Go through the package and see what applies to you. You will need to write a hardship letter explaining to the bank why you want a short sale when your payments are not yet late.

We have been surprised how easy short sales have been lately.

Putting the Package Together

We have discussed in the past few sections different items that will help build a stronger case. Remember, include any item you believe will help you. Even if you don't see it listed here or are in doubt of what to send, simply ask yourself this question, **"Will this item help or hurt my chances of a short sale?"** If the answer is yes, send it. If you come up with anything new, let us know so we can teach others.

Sample Contract for Sale and Purchase

It is easier to get a short sale accepted if you have a signed sales contract. Even if you don't, pursue the short sale while looking for a buyer. Contracts are easy to fill out. If you are working with an investor, send a sales contract with your initial package. If you are trying this one your own, let the loss mitigation representative know that you are looking for a buyer. We explain this contract as we go. You can get a copy of a sample contract on our web site—www.theieu.com—we recommend that you use the contract for your state (Figure 8.2). It can be purchased at the local office supply store.

Sample Comparable Sales

The comps in Figure 8.3 would justify an **initial offer** on a property worth between $200,000 and $250,000. By showing QC (quit claim deed), SW (special warranty deed), and CT (certificate of title), the banks sees what you see—an unstable area. These types of deeds are typically tied to a distressed property. SW and QC are usually deeds from a sheriff's sale. A warranty deed typically shows a normal closing.

Your real estate agent can pull deed types for you. Not all states offer this in the comparable sales, but many do. We love it when we can use deed types as a negotiating tool. It shows distress in the area, foreclosures, deaths, divorces, and more. It helps to project instability in the area, which helps you get a better short sale.

If for some reason you cannot find any low comps, then leave them out. Remember, everything either helps you or hurts you in the short sale process. High comparable sales will not help.

In a short sale, the bank needs to step in and become the seller. Otherwise, you—the distressed seller—have to come up with money to close. Since this is a short sale, we assume you have no money and need to push these expenses over to the bank. Otherwise, whoever is buying from you will have to pay these expenses. Banks typically will pay closing costs.

Sample Pictures of Disrepair

Figures 8.4 through 8.5 show some pictures of a few different properties we have worked on. We realize that many of your houses do not look like this, but some will. It is easy to let a house go when the emotional toll takes over. The bigger the emotional burden, the less likely you are to fix things because you really just don't care anymore.

Send pictures only if they help your case. If your house looks like the cover of *Home and Garden,* don't send photos.

Sample Net Sheet

In most short sales, the bank will want to see in advance how much money it will net after all the closing costs have been paid. Since you are facing financial hardship, you want the bank or the new buyer to pay ALL of the closing costs. If you do not get the bank or new buyer to agree to pay the closing costs, you may have to come to the closing with money. Not something we want to see you do.

Figure 8.7 is a sample net sheet. Look how many of the closing costs typically go to the distressed homeowner. You want to make sure either the bank or the person buying your property pay for everything.

Sample Investor Letter

If you use the services of a real estate investor, look over our sample letter (Figure 8.8). Investors always write an introduction letter to the bank. Have your investors show you the letter they intend to use. It needs to cover why they want the short sale, the repairs the property needs, and that you suffer no tax consequences.

Investors are not used to educated homeowners so they may be taken back, at first, by your request. Do not be shy about asking for copies of the short sale package. This is *your* house and *your* chance to start over. Take control of it.

Sample Repair List

A repair list is always helpful. Any repairs the property needs will have to be done by the bank before the bank can sell the property for retail value. If the bank chooses not to do the necessary repairs, it will have to sell the property for less—something in your favor.

Our repair list, Figure 8.9, covers many repairs a property might need. Try to be as detailed as possible. The larger the repair list, the deeper the discount.

Making Sure Your Package Is Complete

Sometimes the bank will ask for additional information before considering your offer. We send such a good package that it rarely happens, but we want you to be aware in case it happens to you.

Think of it like this: You have a checklist of items you are sending to the bank in hopes of an acceptance (Figure 8.10). The bank also has a checklist of items it needs in order to give you a yes.

You send:

➤ A sales contract.
➤ A net sheet.
➤ A hardship letter.
➤ Comps.
➤ Your cover letter.
➤ List of repairs.
➤ Nasty pictures.

The bank has a checklist with these items on it:

➤ Listing agreement.
➤ Financial hardship package.
➤ Net sheet.
➤ Sales contract.

Notice that in your package you did not include two items: the listing agreement and the financial hardship package.

Because these two items are missing, you might get a "no" without knowing why.

By sending the additional information—hardship letter, pictures, list of repairs, and comps—you might get a bigger discount because you built a better case.

In addition to meeting its own checklist, when the bank asks for additional information, it is often to appease shareholders. Every property you negotiate has a mortgage that is part of a larger package. Each of these packages has investors or shareholders who make the final decision as to whether to short sale. Some shareholders will short sale; some will not. When your loss mitigation representative asks for more information, it is to show the shareholders why they should accept your offer. A sheet that coordinates the deal (Figure 8.11) can be helpful to keep all the facts in front of you.

With luck and persistence, you should get your offer accepted. Almost every bank will accept a short sale; the key is getting it low enough to make it a good deal so you can start over.

The key is always to ask the loss mitigation representative if there is anything at all that you can send to help the representative get a yes. The goal of loss mitigation is to get a yes—to get rid of losses for the bank. A good package gets a yes.

Sample Short Sale Package

The following pages contain sample forms for a short sale.

FIGURE 8.1   Sample Proof of Financial Hardship (Downloadable*)

	Monthly Expenses		Copies Provided	End of Month Cash Flow	
Itemized List	Itemized Income ($)	Itemized List	Itemized Expense ($)		Difference ($)
Salary	3,000	Mortgage	1,200	Yes	
Child support	0	Insurance	200	Yes	
Part-time job	0	RE Taxes	200	Yes	
Annuities	0	Car payments	375	Yes	
Alimony	0	Car insurance	120	Yes	
Other: Please list	0	Groceries	350	No	
		Medical	100	Yes	
		Utilities	250	Yes	
		Credit card payments	200	Yes	
		Clothing	0	No	
		Entertainment	0	No	
		School supplies	0	No	
		Emergencies	0		
Total income	3,000	Total expenses	2,995		5

*Copyright © 2009 by Dwan-Bent Twyford and Bill Twyford. To download and customize this form for your personal use, please visit www.theieu.com/underwaterform.

FIGURE 8.2   Contract for Sale and Purchase (Downloadable*)

Seller _____ with a property located at _____ and Buyer (who you are selling the property to), with an address of _____, do hereby agree that the Seller shall sell and the Buyer shall buy the following property **upon the terms and conditions hereinafter set forth,** which shall include the **standards for real estate transactions** set forth within this contract.

☞ **In this section, check all items that will remain with the property:**   Personal property included: All fixed equipment; all window screens, treatments, and hardware; all wall-to-wall floor coverings; attached wall coverings, and attached lighting fixtures as now installed on said property. Also included are the indicated major appliances: range _____, refrigerator _____, dishwasher _____, disposal _____, microwave oven _____, trash compactor _____, washer _____, dryer _____.

Additional personal property included: _____

1. LEGAL DESCRIPTION of real estate located in _____ County, State of _____:

Legal description:

_____

_____

☞ **Get a deposit from the buyer of at least $3,000.**

2. PURCHASE PRICE $ _____

(a) Deposit $_____

Deposit to be held in trust by: YOUR CLOSING AGENT

(b) Additional deposit due within _____ days after date of acceptance. Time is of the essence as to additional deposit. $ _____

☞ **In this section, mark everything n/a. We are not accepting contracts based on financing.**

(c) Amount of new note and mortgage to be executed by the Buyer to any Lender other than the Seller. New note to be adjustable rate _____ or fixed rate _____. $_____

FHA _____ VA _____ (if applicable)

(continued)

FIGURE 8.2 *(Continued)*

(d) Approximate additional payment due at closing in U.S. currency or LOCAL cashier's check (does not include buyer's closing costs and/or prepaid items). $ _____

3. PRORATIONS: Taxes, insurance, interest, rents, and other expenses and revenue of said property shall be prorated as of the date of closing.

4. RESTRICTIONS, EASEMENTS, LIMITATIONS: Buyer shall take title subject to: (a) Zoning, restrictions, prohibitions and requirements imposed by governmental authority; (b) Restrictions and matters appearing on the plat or common to the subdivision; (c) Public utility easements of record, provided said easements are located on the side or rear lines of the property; (d) Taxes for year of closing, assumed mortgages, and purchase money mortgages, if any; (e) Other _____.

Seller warrants that there shall be no violations of building or zoning codes at the time of closing.

5. DEFAULT BY BUYER: If the Buyer fails to perform any of the covenants of this contract, all money paid pursuant to this contract by Buyer as previously mentioned shall be retained by or for the account of the Seller as consideration for the execution of this contract and as agreed liquidated damages and in full settlement of any claims for damages.

6. DEFAULT BY SELLER: If the Seller fails to perform any of the covenants of this contract, the aforesaid money paid by the Buyer, at the option of the Buyer, shall be returned to the Buyer on demand; or the Buyer shall have only the right of liquidated damages.

7. TERMITE INSPECTION: At least 15 days before closing, Buyer, at Buyer's expense, shall have the right to obtain a written report from a licensed exterminator stating that there is no evidence of live termite or other wood boring insect infestation on said property nor substantial damage from prior infestation on said property. If there is such evidence, Seller shall pay up to two (2%) percent of the purchase price for the treatment required to remedy such infestation, including repairing and replacing portions of said improvements which have been damaged; but if the costs for such treatment or repairs exceed three (3%) percent of the

FIGURE 8.2   *(Continued)*

purchase price, Buyer may elect to pay such excess. If Buyer elects not to pay, Seller may pay the excess or cancel the contract.

8. ROOF INSPECTION: At least 15 days before closing, Buyer, at Buyer's expense, shall have the right to obtain a written report from a licensed roofer stating that the roof is in a watertight condition. In the event repairs are required either to correct leaks or to repair damage to fascia or soffit, Seller shall pay up to two (2%) percent of the purchase price for said repairs which shall be performed by a licensed roofing contractor; but if the costs for such repairs exceeds three (3%) percent of the purchase price, Buyer may elect to pay such excess. If Buyer elects not to pay, Seller may pay the excess or cancel the contract.

9. OTHER INSPECTIONS: At least 15 days before closing, Buyer or his agent may inspect all appliances, air conditioning and heating systems, electrical systems, plumbing, machinery, sprinklers and pool system included in the sale. Seller shall pay for the repairs necessary to place such items in working order at the time of closing. Within 48 hours before closing, Buyer shall be entitled, upon reasonable notice to Seller, to inspect the premises to determine that said items are in working order. All items of personal property included in the sale shall be transferred by Bill of Sale with warranty of title.

10. LEASES: Seller, not less than 15 days before closing, shall furnish to Buyer copies of all written leases and estoppel letters from each tenant specifying the nature and duration of the tenant's occupancy, rental rates, and advanced rent and security deposits paid by tenant. If Seller is unable to obtain such letters from tenants, Seller shall furnish the same information to Buyer within said time period in the form of a Seller's affidavit, and Buyer may contact tenants thereafter to confirm such information. At closing, Seller shall deliver and assign all original leases to Buyer.

11. MECHANICS' LIENS: Seller shall furnish to Buyer an affidavit that there have been no improvements to the subject property for 90 days immediately preceding the date of closing, and no financing statements,

(continued)

FIGURE 8.2   *(Continued)*

claims of lien or potential lienors known to Seller. If the property has been improved within that time, Seller shall deliver releases or waivers of all mechanics' liens as executed by general contractors, subcontractors, suppliers, and material men and reciting that all bills for work to the subject property which could serve as basis for mechanics' liens have been paid or will be paid at closing.

12. PLACE OF CLOSING: Closing shall be held at the office of the Seller's attorney or as otherwise agreed on.

13. TIME IS OF THE ESSENCE: Time is of the essence of this Sale and Purchase Agreement.

14. DOCUMENTS FOR CLOSING: Seller's attorney shall prepare deed, note, mortgage, Seller's affidavit, any corrective instruments required for perfecting the title, and closing statement, and submit copies of same to Buyer's attorney, and copy of closing statement to the broker, at least two days prior to scheduled closing date.

15. EXPENSES: State documentary stamps required on the instrument of conveyance and the cost of recording any corrective instruments shall be paid by Seller. Documentary stamps to be affixed to the note secured by the purchase money mortgage shall be paid by Buyer.

16. INSURANCE: If insurance is to be prorated, the Seller shall on or before the closing date, furnish to Buyer all insurance policies or copies thereof.

17. RISK OF LOSS: If the improvements are damage by fire or causality before delivery of the deed and can be restored to substantiality the same condition as now within a period of 60 days thereafter, Seller shall so restore the improvements and the closing date and date of delivery of possession herein provided shall be extended accordingly. If Seller fails to do so, the Buyer shall have the option of (1) taking the property as-is, together with insurance proceeds, if any, or (2) canceling the contract, and all deposits shall be forthwith returned to the Buyer and all parties shall be released of any and all obligations and liability.

FIGURE 8.2   (Continued)

18. MAINTENANCE: Between the date of the contract and the date of closing, the property, including lawn, shrubbery, and pool, if any, shall be maintained by Seller in the condition as it existed as of the date of the contract, ordinary wear and tear excepted.

19. CLOSING DATE: This contract shall be closed and the deed and possession shall be delivered on or before the _____ day of _____, unless extended by other provisions of this contract.

20. TYPEWRITTEN OR HANDWRITTEN PROVISIONS: Typewritten or handwritten provisions inserted in this form shall control all printed provisions in conflict therewith.

21. SPECIAL CLAUSES:

_____

_____

COMMISSION TO BROKER: The Seller hereby recognizes _____ as the Broker in this transaction, and agrees to pay as commission _____% of the gross sales price, or the sum of _____ dollars ($_____), or one-half of the deposit in case same is forfeited by the Buyer through failure to perform, as compensation for services rendered, provided same does not exceed the full amount of the commission.

SIGNATURES:

_____	_____
BUYER	DATE
_____	_____
BUYER	DATE
_____	_____
WITNESS	DATE
_____	_____
SELLER	DATE
_____	_____
SELLER	DATE
_____	_____
WITNESS	DATE

FIGURE 8.3   Sample Area Comps (Downloadable*)

Your Name

719 Robin Road

City of Subject Property

Zip Code

List the past two sale prices of your property. If you don't know what the person before you paid—have a real estate agent look it up for you.

Recent Sales	Amount ($)	Deed Type
926 Hummingbird Lane	139,000	WD
267 Robin Road	135,000	CT
687 Blue Jay Lane	129,000	CT
567 Blue Jay Lane	99,000	SW
126 Crow Street	135,000	QC
851 Eagle Road	137,000	WD

*Copyright © 2009 by Dwan-Bent Twyford and Bill Twyford. To download and customize this form for your personal use, please visit www.theieu.com/underwaterform.

FIGURE 8.4   Home Exterior

FIGURE 8.5   Large Kitchen

FIGURE 8.6   Kitchen Close Up

FIGURE 8.7   Sample Net Sheet (Downloadable*)

Total Expenses	Dollar Amount ($)	Expense for the Bank	Expense for the Buyer	Expense for the Seller
Property Sales Price: $225,000				
Doc stamps	1,800			X
Real estate taxes	3,000			X
Document preparation	300		X	
Wiring fees	50			X
Property insurance	1,200		X	
Real estate commission	13,500			X
Cash in from buyer	22,500		X	
Cash out to seller	0			
Title insurance	350			X
Total Expenses				

*Copyright © 2009 by Dwan-Bent Twyford and Bill Twyford. To download and customize this form for your personal use, please visit www.theieu.com/underwaterform.

FIGURE 8.8   Sample Investor Introduction Letter (Downloadable*)

Dear Mrs. Banker: June 1

I am interested in buying the property located at 516 West Tree Street. **During a room-by-room inspection, I was shocked to see the damage to the property.** My contractor and I estimate the cost to bring the property to current market condition to be in the neighborhood of $40,000 to $45,000.

This includes:

New roof	$ 8,000
Carpet	7,500
Water damage repair	11,500
Painting interior	6,500
Repair ext. steps/deck/paint	8,750
Total	$ 42,250

My real estate agent says the property would be worth between $78,000 and $80,000 if it were in mint condition. Based on current market, the poor condition of the property, and the extensive repairs needed, I have offered Distressed Homeowners $27,750 as payment in full.

Mrs. Banker, this offer is net to your investors. After your investors see the pictures and do the walk-through, you'll know you made the right decision by taking this offer. I will close on or before June 15.

Prices in this area have taken several tumbles the last six months. **The headlines in your local paper stated, "Foreclosures at an all time high ... up 200% from last year."** The article is enclosed.

I feel this offer is more than fair, and I urge you to accept it as well as **waive any deficiency judgment against the Distressed Homeowner.** I hope we can work together. You can call my office at 555-222-7777 anytime.

Sincerely,

Mr. Investor

FIGURE 8.9   Sample Repair List (Downloadable*)

COMPLETE REPAIR LIST	COST	REPAIR TIME-FRAME
Roof – fascia, wood rot, removal, replacement, etc.		
Paint – Exterior		
Paint – Interior		
Debris Removal		
Electrical		
Plumbing		
Flooring		
Windows		
Heat & Air Conditioning		
Landscaping		
Exterior Doors		
Interior Doors		
Bathrooms		
Kitchen		
Possible Code Violations		
Fencing and Exterior Work		
Permits		
TOTAL EXPENSES - TIME-FRAME		

FIGURE 8.10 Sample Short Sale Checklist (Downloadable*)

Items Required by Bank	Check if Included	Additional Items We Send to Build a Stronger Case	Check if Included
Financial hardship package		Nonpayment of alimony	
Tax returns		Hardship letter	
Paycheck stubs		Proof of hardship	
Bank statements		Pictures of disrepair	
Copy of late notices		Proof of declining 401K	
Sales contract		Proof of using savings to live	
Net sheet		Proof of job loss	
Credit card payments		Proof of divorce	
Comparable sales		Proof of probate	
Listing agreement		Pawnshop tickets	
Proof of funds		Met the agent for BPO	
Scheduled a BPO		Crime reports	
Detailed list of repairs		Sex offenders	
		Market changes	
		Pictures of boarded up houses	
		Pictures of new construction	
		Mold test kit	
Other:		Other:	

FIGURE 8.11   Sample Deal Coordinating Sheet (Downloadable*)

When we work on more than one short sale, we use this form to keep track of who everyone is. When working on 15 or 20 short sales at once all the different people seem to run together. You will find this form helpful, especially if this is your first short sale. Whether you do just this one, are a full-time investor now, or decide to help homeowners for a living, keeping track of the different players, the different calls, faxes, emails, and more is crucial to your deal. You certainly don't want to call loss mitigation and forget where you are in your deal.

Date: _____

PROPERTY ADDRESS: _____

_____

PURCHASE PRICE $_____

Listing Agent: _____

Email: _____

Cell Ph: _____ Office Ph: _____ Fax: _____

Buyer's Agent: _____

Email: _____

Cell Ph: _____ Office Ph: _____ Fax: _____

Owner or Seller: _____

Email: _____

Cell Ph: _____ Office Ph: _____ Fax: _____

Short Sale Bank Name(s): _____

Email: _____

Cell Ph: _____ Office Ph: _____ Fax: _____

End Buyer: _____

Proof of Funds: _____

Email: _____

Cell Ph: _____ Office Ph: _____ Fax: _____

(continued)

FIGURE 8.11   (Continued)

Closing Information:

Title Company #1: _____

Contact: _____

Office Ph: _____ Fax: _____

Email: _____

Buyers Mortgage Broker/Lender: _____

Cell Ph: _____ Office Ph: _____

Fax: _____ Loan info: _____

Sellers Lender: _____

Cell Ph: _____ Office Ph: _____

Fax: _____ Loan info: _____

Real Estate Commissions Due:

Realty & Fee: _____

Assignment Fee: _____

Consulting Fee: _____

BACK UP OFFERS: _____

Straight Sale: _____ Assignment: _____ Double Closing: _____

Closing Date:_____ Time:_____ Location: _____

CHAPTER 9

How to Work with an Ethical Investor to Short Sale a Property

There are still some banks that do not allow homeowners to short sale their own properties. Unfortunately, we can't give you a list of those banks because it changes every day. As an individual homeowner or an investor with upside-down properties, you may have to find an investor to work with you. We want to make sure you find someone with very high ethics because you are in a very vulnerable state right now and it would be easy for someone to take advantage of you and take your house.

Here's the weird part—we typically teach investors how to find distressed sellers and how to make sure the homeowner does not take advantage of the investor. We cover, in detail, how ethical investors must be in order to work with us. Now we are teaching homeowners how to qualify investors—something investors are not used to. Investors are used to qualifying homeowners. There is nothing worse than working on a deal for two months and then the homeowners decide to work with your competitor instead of you because the other investor offered the homeowners more money. Remember—if other investors will cut us out, why would they pay you? You will get cut out, but only after it is too late. We have seen it happen hundreds of times. So, we are going to walk on the other side of the fence and teach you how to qualify investors.

Unfortunately, there are plenty of unethical players in this business. Every business in the world has its fair share of them—we want to make certain you have a pleasant experience.

The number one thing to remember is to make sure investors put everything in writing and that the investors do not ask you to deed your property to them. Once you give up the deed, you have given up all your rights. In Chapter 7, we talked about a *deed in lieu of foreclosure*. If this is the option you chose, you will be giving up all your rights to the property as soon as you turn your deed over to someone else.

Deeding your house to someone is a very big decision and should not be taken lightly. Many investors will tell you to deed the property to them so that they can negotiate with the bank. **No one needs a deed to negotiate with a bank.** All the bank needs is an "Authorization to Release Information" form signed by you...that's it (Figure 9.1).

What Should an Investor Do for Me?

It is important to remember that investors do not work for free. Just like you, investors have bills to pay. We think investors should get paid a fair wage for what they do, without going overboard. An investor has to:

➤ Find the distressed seller.
➤ Do all the paperwork necessary to create a short sale package.
➤ Negotiate with the bank on your behalf.
➤ Find a buyer or arrange funds to purchase the property themselves.
➤ Find a title company.
➤ Close on the property before you lose it at the sheriff's sale.
➤ Rehab the property or flip it to a rehabber or landlord.
➤ Possibly put it back on the market and try to sell it for a profit and much more behind-the-scenes work.

FIGURE 9.1 Authorization to Release Information (Downloadable*)

To Whom It May Concern:

I give my permission for you to release any and all information to THE INVESTOR regarding my property located at "1279 Smith Street, Dayton, Ohio 45388" in reference to any mortgage(s), liens, judgments, or bankruptcy proceedings as well as my personal information including medical or credit information.

BORROWER _____

CO-BORROWER _____

Borrower _____

Address _____

City _____ St _____ Zip _____

Home Phone _____ Cell _____

S.S. No. _____

Mortgagee _____

Phone _____ Fax _____

Email _____

Loan No. _____

Contact _____

SIGNATURES: _____

SIGNATURES: _____

*Copyright © 2009 by Dwan-Bent Twyford and Bill Twyford. To download and customize this form for your personal use, please visit www.theieu.com/underwaterform.

The investor does not get paid a dime unless the short sale is accepted and the deal is closed. Many investors work on properties for three or four months only to have the bank say no and lose the deal. Do not work with an investor who wants money up-front in order to work with you. We *never* ask for money up-front. We get paid **if** we perform.

Typically, we get paid between 10 percent and 20 percent of the value of the property. For example, if we were to work on a $200,000 property, we would get paid between $20,000 and $40,000 depending on how deep we were able to short sale the property. Assume we were making $25,000 on a deal. We would still have to pay closing costs and whatever dollar amount we have agreed to pay the homeowners.

Remember the "Bill of Sale" we gave you in Chapter 5? This is where you would use it. The investor would buy something from you, give you the cash, and use a bill of sale for the transaction. This meets the bank's requirements of you not getting any sale proceeds (we'll talk about that later) and still gives you cash in your pocket to operate with. Never work with any investor who says there is not enough money in the deal for you. We have done many deals and made zero in order to give the homeowners money. Because we work with homeowners for a living, we know there is always another deal around the corner and that this is the homeowner's one chance to get a fresh start. The homeowners must come first! Do not work with anyone who does not put you first.

Because this may be the first time you have ever worked with an investor, you need to find a good one. Start by running an ad in the paper (see Figure 9.2).

We realize that it may be unnerving to run an ad like this. This is the exact ad we run every time we get a house under contract. We are wholesalers. We get houses under contract, negotiate the short sale, and then sell the house to another investor who either rehabs it or keeps it for a rental. We have used this ad for years with great success. Your goal is to get as many investors as possible to interview.

An ad like this will cause your phone to ring off the hook. As soon as it does, begin to interview investors, make appointments with several different ones, and then work with the investor who will answer your questions and use a Homeowner

FIGURE 9.2   Sample Ad

I have a house in foreclosure.

Please help!

... your phone number here ...

Protection Agreement (Figure 9.3). Many investors won't put everything in writing. These are the ones you are trying to avoid.

For many years now, we have asked homeowners to sign this agreement. We have never had a single homeowner ask us to do it. We are curious to see how investors will feel when the roles are reversed. By the way, we have thousands and thousands of students nationwide so it is possible you may come across one of them. If you do, they will ask you to sign this agreement. Wouldn't that be great to have one of our highly trained students be the person who calls you for help? You wouldn't have to worry about a thing.

Put It in Writing—The Homeowners Protection Agreement

After seeing so many investors on the front page of the newspaper over the years, we decided to start putting everything in writing. This avoids the he said/she said part of life. All of us tend to hear what we want to hear and only remember what is convenient for us. That is not a cut on anyone—we all do it. When working with someone in distress or someone who could take advantage of someone in distress, putting it in writing protects all parties. You would not send this agreement to the bank. It is between you and the investor. The agreement in Figure 9.3 is an agreement to agree.

This is a thorough document. It protects the investor as well as you. You are agreeing to agree. You can't go around the investor and the investor can't go around you. The investor isn't taking the deed to your house and then kicking you out. Everyone agrees on the sales price, that a short sale must be done; you have the option to take cash now and waive further rights or take a percentage once a short sale is completed. It's a good agreement for all parties concerned.

Investors will be stunned that you have something like this. By using this agreement along with a Purchase and Sale Contract, everyone is on the same page. That is the beginning of a wonderful working relationship.

Once the bank agrees to the short sale, it will send the investor an acceptance letter—included in Chapter 10. In every

FIGURE 9.3 Homeowner Protection Agreement (Downloadable*)

Affidavit of this agreement is not an addendum to purchase agreement dated _____, 20_____

THIS IS AN IMPORTANT LEGAL CONTRACT CONCERNING THE SALE OF MY HOME AND SHOULD BE READ CAREFULLY. CONTACT AN ATTORNEY BEFORE SIGNING.

STATE OF _____)

COUNTY OF _____)

THIS AGREEMENT (hereinafter referred to as the "Agreement"), becomes effective on_____,_____ 200 _____, by _____ and _____ hereinafter referred to as "Seller(s)," and _____ hereinafter referred to as "Buyer."

Property location for Seller(s):

_____

Address

_____

City, State, Zip

_____

Home Number

_____

Cell Phone Number

_____

Work Number   Fax Number

_____   _____

Buyer's business address:

_____

Address

_____

City, State, Zip

FIGURE 9.3   *(Continued)*

Office Number

_____

Cell Phone Number   Fax Number

_____   _____

Nature of this Agreement: Marketing, selling, and distribution of all funds (including deduction of expenses) for the above referenced property.

Duration of this Agreement: This Agreement remains in full force and effect until the completion and distribution of all funds, including the successful closing of the above referenced property.

5.   Applicable to Successors: This Agreement and each provision herein shall be binding upon and applicable to, and shall inure to the benefit of, the parties hereto and their respective heirs, legatees, successors, assigns and legal representatives, except as otherwise expressly provided herein.

Contribution of Capital: Each seller(s) shall contribute capital and additional resources as follows:

____Buyer_____ is responsible for all expertise in sales and marketing the above referenced property.

_____Buyer_____ is responsible for taking care of all research and legal forms relating to the payoff from the Foreclosure Attorney.

____Seller_____ and _____Seller_____ will sign an Authorization to Release form in order that _____ Buyer _____ can negotiate with the Bank or Mortgage Company on their behalf.

Appropriation of Expenses: The following represent expenses associated with the sale of the above referenced property.

Payoff with Foreclosure Attorney

Title Insurance

Unpaid Property taxes

Interest on Capital

Closing Costs

(continued)

FIGURE 9.3   (*Continued*)

Lender Fees

Recording Fees

Liens and Judgments

Cost of Realtor (if involved 3%)

Marketing and selling costs to _____Buyer_____and/or assigns of (10% of the sales price).

Code Violations

H.O.A. Fees

Please note "all unforeseen expenses" that arise will be added to expenses.

Profits and Losses: Net profits of this Agreement will be divided proportionately between the parties as follows:

_____Seller_____ and _____ Seller _____ will receive _____% upon a successful closing after all expenses are paid. If a Short Sale is worked out with the mortgage company then the Seller(s) will receive no profits from this transaction.

Buyer has the right to buy whatever Seller(s) want to sell. A "Bill of Sale" will be used for this sale.

Seller(s) _____   Buyer_____

9.   Termination of this Agreement: This Agreement will only terminate upon the completion and distribution of all funds, including the successful closing of the above referenced property.

10.   I/We _____ Seller(s) waive my/our right to the _____% of equity today and any other future equity that the buyer creates by taking the $ _____ cash on or before this _____ day of _____, 200___.

I/We will vacate the property located at _____ on or before _____.

My/Our initials attest to my/our understanding and acceptance of paragraph 10:

Seller(s) _____   Buyer_____

FIGURE 9.3 *(Continued)*

11. Both Buyer and Seller(s) agree that according to the condition of said property, and the poor market value, and the Seller(s)situation, said property is worth between $_____ and $_____.

My/Our initials attest to my/our understanding and acceptance of paragraph 11:

Seller(s) _____   Buyer_____

12. Seller(s) understand and accept that they may have to sell the said property "BELOW MARKET VALUE" to avoid foreclosure proceedings. The sale price will be a joint decision between Buyer and Seller(s).

My/Our initials attest to my/our understanding and acceptance of paragraph 12:

Seller(s) _____   Buyer_____

13. Seller(s) are currently in default of their loan(s) and are unable to make up their back payments or continue making further payments. They have attempted several other avenues of action to remedy their financial situation, including:

_____

_____

_____

_____

My/Our initials attest to my/our understanding and acceptance of paragraph 13:

Seller(s) _____   Buyer_____

14. The Buyer may attempt to negotiate a Short Sale with the bank(s). Buyer has not made me any promises, guarantees or representations about his ability to complete this task, save my credit, or stop the foreclosure process. I understand fully and completely that if purchaser is not able to negotiate the short sale with the lender, the lenders may proceed with foreclosure.

(continued)

FIGURE 9.3   (Continued)

I further understand that if the lender accepts a short sale, this may or may not relieve me of my personal responsibility for the loan and may affect my credit score. I also understand that any forbearance or forgiveness of debt by lien holders may result in a taxable gain and I should consult with a qualified tax advisor to discuss the implications of such a gain if I should receive a form 1099 from the lender.

My/Our initials attest to my/our understanding and acceptance of paragraph 14:

Seller(s) _____   Buyer_____

15.   I agree to waive any rights I may have to any prepaid or escrowed property taxes, insurance, homeowner's association dues, county property tax refunds or other amounts held by any party in escrow, including, but not limited to lenders, homeowner's associations, and insurance companies.

Seller(s) _____   Buyer_____

16.   I have had the opportunity to seek legal, tax, and financial counsel as to this transaction. I understand that the Buyer is not my agent, representative, or real estate agent in this transaction and is not acting on my behalf. The Buyer has made no representations as to seller's legal rights or options with regard to his property. I UNDERSTAND THAT THIS DOCUMENT DOES NOT DEFINE OR EXPLAIN MY RIGHTS OR OPTIONS, and I have had the opportunity to seek legal, financial, tax, or other professional counsel to weigh my options, my rights, and the legal consequences of this transaction.

Seller(s) _____   Buyer_____

17.   I understand that this agreement is a negotiated sale of my property, even though my existing loan(s) may not be paid off. I understand that this transaction creates a "sale," for state and federal income tax purposes and that I have had the opportunity to review these tax implications with a qualified tax advisor.

Seller(s) _____   Buyer_____

FIGURE 9.3 *(Continued)*

18. I understand Buyer may assign the Purchase Agreement to another party for a profit and that I may be closing the sale with someone other than Buyer. I also understand Buyer may close in the name of a nominee or related company or may choose to resell the property to another party for a profit.

Seller(s) _____   Buyer_____

19. Buyer agrees to provide me with copies of documents I have signed within 2 (two) business days of this agreement. I may request additional copies of said documents at any time by paying the cost of reproduction.

Seller(s) _____   Buyer_____

20. I understand that I may have certain rights under the state or federal law, including, but not limited to bankruptcy, redemption, or other equitable rights that may give me additional rights to equity or continued possession of the property. This disclosure is not to be construed as a list of my rights or legal advice, but simply an acknowledgment that I have investigated my rights under the law.

Seller(s) _____   Buyer_____

21. I understand by signing the Purchase and Sale Contract, I have agreed to sell the Property to the Buyer and I am now bound by the terms and conditions described in that Agreement. I further understand that I cannot continue to market the Property to any other party, except as provided herein.

Seller(s) _____   Buyer_____

22. The Buyer has agreed to give me $ _____ on or about _____, 20___, which is fair and adequate consideration for my rights in the property, even though this may be less than what I could expect to gain from either curing the loan and/or negotiating a workout or forbearance or modification with my lender and/or refinancing the debt and/or placing the property for sale on the open marketplace either myself or through a real estate broker and that I am knowingly and willingly agreeing to accept this consideration knowing these options and other potential options are available to me.

Seller(s) _____   Buyer_____

(continued)

FIGURE 9.3   (*Continued*)

23.   I understand that the Buyer is not acting on my behalf as counselor, advisor, consultant, or nonprofit agency. I understand that Buyer may make a substantial profit from this transaction and that his primary motivation in engaging in this transaction is to make a profit from the rental or resale of the property.

Seller(s) _____   Buyer_____

24.   I am not under the influence of alcohol, drugs, or any other ailment at this time that would affect my ability to read this document and make an intelligent decision as to the consequences of signing it.

Seller(s) _____   Buyer_____

25.   In the event a dispute arises between any Parties, the prevailing party shall be entitled to recover reasonable attorney's fees and court costs incurred. The venue for court will be in the County of _____ State of _____ or deemed by Buyer and/or assigns.

26.   In the event that any paragraph in this contract is deemed not to be legal in the State of _____ then that paragraph is the only paragraph that will be voided not the entire contract.

27.   Seller agrees that English is his/her first language by initializing paragraph 16.

Seller(s) _____   Buyer_____

Concerns or objections to this agreement from Seller

_____

_____

_____

Signed and Entered into this Agreement with

_____ Buyer and/or assigns on this the _____ day of _____, 200___.

_____

Buyer

_____

Seller

_____

FIGURE 9.3   (*Continued*)

Seller

State of _____§

County of _____§

Sworn and Subscribed to me by _____Seller_____ and

_____Seller_____, who personally executed the

foregoing Equity Agreement before me (a notary public) on this the _____

day of _____, 200___.

_____

Notary Public

My commission expires on_____

State of _____§

County of _____§

Sworn and Subscribed to me by _____Buyer_____ and

_____Buyer_____, who personally executed the foregoing

Equity Agreement before me (a notary public) on this the _____ day of

_____, 200___.

_____

Notary Public   My commission expires

on_____

*Copyright © 2009 by Dwan-Bent Twyford and Bill Twyford. To download and customize this form for your personal use, please visit www.theieu.com/underwaterform.

acceptance letter the bank states that the homeowners are to "receive no proceeds" from the sale of the property. Although we sign the Homeowner Protection Agreement with our homeowners, we go one-step further. We buy something from them, give them a Bill of Sale (Figure 9.4), and make sure that they have enough money to get started with. Since the bank does not want us to give them money, we buy something from them.

How to Negotiate with Investors

The first step you are going to take is to interview investors to see who is the best fit for you and your situation. Remember,

FIGURE 9.4   Sample Bill of Sale (Downloadable*)

This is a bill of sale for the following exchange of goods:

_____ (Buyer), in the county of _____,

in the state of _____, for ten dollars and other good and valuable

consideration, paid _____ (Seller) in the county of

_____, in the state of _____.

This receipt, of which is hereby acknowledged, has bargained and sold the following property and/or goods:

_____

_____

For a value of:

_____

_____

_____

Buyer   Date

_____

_____

Seller   Date

In witness whereof, the Seller has executed this Bill of Sale this _____

day of _____, in the year _____.

Notary Public: _____ Commission expires:

_____

*Copyright © 2009 by Dwan-Bent Twyford and Bill Twyford. To download and customize this form for your personal use, please visit www.theieu.com/underwaterform.

when an investor calls you, the investor is going to try to be in control of the conversation. Inform them that you read a book by Bill and Dwan Twyford and that you are going to interview them. Even if you are an investor who is upside down, take control of the conversation. We teach our students to be in control of everything so that the deal does not fall apart. When you are the one in trouble, you need to be in control of the deal so that it does not fall apart. If you run across one of our students, they will know us and be thrilled to work with you.

When an investor calls, here is the basic script:

You: Hello.

Them: I saw your ad in the paper stating that you have a house in foreclosure.

You: Yes, I do. Who am I speaking to?

Them: [They will state their name.]

You: Hi—Investor—my name is _____. Why did you call?

Them: I work with people in distress and I want to help. Can you tell me a little about your house?

You: Let me tell you a little about my situation first (explain hardship here—I lost my job, got sick, going through a divorce, losing my rentals, and so on). I've already contacted my bank and tried to do a short sale. The bank said that it won't work directly with me and that I need a third party. So I am interviewing investors for the job of doing a short sale on my property and then buying it. I'd like to ask you a few questions:

➤ How long have you been investing?

➤ Do you have any reference letters from other homeowners?

➤ How many short sales have you done?

➤ Please tell me about the last one you did? (Because you have read this book, you'll know by what they say if they have actually done a short sale.)

➤ Do you have a reference letter from the last bank you did a short sale with? Can you get one?

➤ Tell me about your typical short sale transaction.

➤ How much money are you looking to make from this deal?

➤ Are you going to personally purchase my house or are you going to wholesale it to another investor? If so, do you have other investors lined up?

➤ I am looking to get out from under this house as soon as possible and want to work with whomever can get the deal done the fastest, easiest way possible. Why should I work with you?

➤ One last thing . . . are you willing to put 100 percent of what
we speak about in writing? Great, I have a Homeowner
Protection Agreement that I want to fax to you so that you
can review it before we meet. I must have it signed before
we can proceed. My coaches said never to work with an
investor who wants my deed or won't put things in writing,
so if you can agree to that, we can meet. Is tonight at 7 or
8 better for you?

From an investor's point of view—we'd be thrilled to find
a homeowner who explained everything upfront, was ready to
get the deal done, wanted everything in writing, and had already
called the bank. In fact, we'd probably drop over dead from the
shock.

Be prepared for some resistance from investors. Again,
investors are used to being in control of the conversation and
the situation. Your knowledge will take the investor by surprise,
but it will be a pleasant surprise.

Once you have picked out an investor for the job, use the
Homeowners Protection Agreement in Figure 9.3 to make sure
you are getting the deal you think you are getting.

It is very important once you pick an investor that you stick
with him or her. There really are a lot of unethical people out
there and if someone tries to get you to go around the person
you are working with, they will stick you at the end. The typical
MO of unethical investors is something like this:

They tell you that they can give you more money and
that you need to get out of the contract you currently
have with the other investor. They promise you the moon
and their deal sounds much better than anything you
have heard to date. Even though you have already made
a deal with someone else, the promise of more money is
appealing in your distressed situation. You get out of one
contract and sign another with the unethical investor who
promised more money. Things seem to be rolling right
along and the day of the closing approaches. Typically,
the investor will set the closing date with you very close
to your sheriff's sale with the bank—this is designed to

squeeze you at the end. You're all sitting at the closing table and the unethical investor states that they miscalculated the money and that there is no money for you after all. They give you two crappy choices—take $500 now or lose your house at the sheriff's sale at the end of the week. Because you have no other choices, you take the money and walk away with nothing but $500 and a lot of anger toward investors.

We have seen this happen a hundred times. It makes us sick when it does, but homeowners are partially to blame. They made a deal, the original investor put many hours into the deal, and then the homeowners bailed because they thought another deal was better. Please make a decision as to whom you'd like to work with and then stick to it. Everyone wins in the end this way.

CHAPTER 10

Closing Any Deal—What You Need to Get in Writing

Great news! You were able to work something out, you found a new buyer for your property, and now you are ready to close the transaction. It is always a great day when a closing is set. You are about to be out of trouble, your new life can start, you can start sleeping at night, and life is taking a turn for the better.

If you are still struggling with the fact that you are losing your house, this might not be such a great day. Keep in mind what we have been saying all along—life *will* get better. A fresh start is just what you need. Once you get moved into a new place and unpack, things will get back to normal.

You should be familiar with the concept of a closing because you purchased your property this way. Everyone comes together, signs papers, ownership transfers, and everyone parts ways. Whether doing a deed in lieu, a short sale, or a conventional closing, you need a good closing agent.

You will need to find a title company, an attorney, or an escrow agent depending on where you live. Different states require different people to close on properties. To keep it simple, we will use the term "closing agent" to refer to the person who will close your transaction. The nice thing about using a closing agent is that they do all the work for you. The job of the closing agent is to represent the transaction—not the people.

Because this closing most likely involves some creative financing (a short sale), you need to work with an

investor-friendly closing agent. There is a web site—www.na
tionalreia.com—where you can find a local closing agent who
works specifically with investors. The bank may also refer you
to its closing agent as well.

The closing may not include creative financing if you are
selling directly to an end buyer. However, if you are selling to an
investor and the investor is then wholesaling the property (flipping it to another person for a profit—www.theieu.com—to find
out more about flipping properties), you will need an investor-
friendly closing agent.

Get Everything in Writing from the Bank, Investor, or Real Estate Agent

There are several things that could be happening right now:

- ➤ You might be doing a short sale. If so, the bank should
  have sent you a letter of acceptance stating that it approved
  the short sale. A typical acceptance letter is shown in
  Figure 10.1.
- ➤ You might have decided to do a deed in lieu of foreclosure.
  Again, the bank should have provided something in writing
  stating that it would not place a foreclosure on your credit
  report.
- ➤ You might be doing a loan modification—again—is it in
  writing?
- ➤ Did you work out a forbearance agreement? Is it in writing?
- ➤ Did the bank agree to waive the deficiency or the 1099? Is
  it in writing?
- ➤ If you are working with an investor, did he or she sign the
  Homeowner Protection Agreement?
- ➤ If you listed your house with a real estate agent, is the
  listing agreement signed? Is the sales contract signed by
  the new buyer?
- ➤ If you are an investor, did you get everything signed by
  everyone else?

FIGURE 10.1   Bank Acceptance Letter (Downloadable*)

Dear Mr. Investor:

Please be advised that management has reviewed the request for a short payoff on the above referenced property. We are COUNTERING your offer of $99,460 with our amount of $103,000 as a FINAL NET to <enter approving bank here>. The mortgagor is to receive no funds from this transaction. Upon receipt of the funds, we will release our lien, and waive the deficiency judgment. All fees, including attorney's fees, are incorporated in this amount.

   This offer is good until 09/15. THIS LETTER MUST BE ATTACHED TO OUR CHECK.

   Should you have any questions, please call me at 555-5555.

   Sincerely,

   Successful Investor

---

*Copyright © 2009 by Dwan-Bent Twyford and Bill Twyford. To download and customize this form for your personal use, please visit www.theieu.com/underwaterform.

No matter what you work out with another person, only what is in writing counts. We have had many loss mitigation representatives agree to waive the deficiency judgment against our homeowners and then not put it in writing. We knew that the representative did not have it approved by the bank or it would have been in the package. We refused to close until the letter was faxed to the closing agent. Funny, how the letters always show up signed by the representative, not the boss. As long as they are on the company letterhead, our attorney advises us it is valid.

Bottom Line

Do not schedule a closing until everything is in writing.

   Do not, under any circumstances, sign any type of closing documents until everything you want to see in writing is in writing.

Do not sell your house without the new buyer agreeing to give you some money. You deserve it and no one should expect you to walk away with nothing.

Sadly, during hard times many unethical people come out of the woodwork. We find that most unethical homeowners or investors do not like to put everything in writing. It gives you proof of a bad deal and leaves them open to lawsuits. If the people you have chosen to work with are more than willing to put everything in writing, it should be safe to move forward.

If you are unsure of anything, call the bank to verify what is happening. Contact your attorney to make sure everything is on the up and up. Do not be afraid to ask questions. Never let anyone intimidate you. This is your property and you are the one in control—remember that.

Bank Acceptance Letter

Figure 10.1 shows one of our successful student's acceptance letter. The property was worth $200,000 and the homeowners owed $170,000. The property needed no work at all. The student offered $99,460.

What to Expect from the Closing Agent

If you don't find a closing agent you like using the National REIA web site, ask your real estate agent or the investor you are working with who they use. It is good to know that people you respect use a particular agent that they like well enough to recommend. Meet with the closing agent to discuss how the company can service your needs.

Closing agents handle many items needed for this deal to close smoothly. Here is what you can expect:

> ➤ Agents handle the closing—sometimes called settlements.
> ➤ Agents perform title searches. This is a search, sometimes called an abstract search, through the title of the property

beginning with the original owner and continuing through the current owner.

➤ The title search is performed to locate any unpaid liens or judgments existing against the property.

Occasionally, a lien will be overlooked and for this reason title insurance is available. Once a title search is completed, and if clear, the closing agent will provide an owner with a title insurance policy. This is a policy issued to the new buyer to protect against arising liens or claims of ownership not found in the title search.

Generally, if the new buyer is placing a mortgage against the property in order to purchase it, the mortgage holder will require a mortgagee's title insurance policy, which will be issued to them by the closing agent and paid for by the new buyer. This policy is issued to the mortgage holder to ensure against arising liens not found in the search.

When the closing agent receives a copy of the Contract for Sale and Purchase, it places that deposit in escrow.

An escrow account, also known as a trust account, is a noninterest bearing bank account set up to hold a deposit until the closing occurs.

The closing agent will prepare an escrow letter for the lender. This is a letter stating that a deposit is being held pending a certain contract. In most states, without a deposit being held, no valid contract exists, regardless of signatures.

The closing agent does not represent the seller or the buyer in the transaction and has no duty to protect their interest.

The closing agent is being hired for this transaction.

In order to fully protect your rights as a seller or a buyer, hire an attorney.

As the closing nears, the title search will be completed and a title commitment will be issued to the lender. This is a commitment to the lender that title is clear and a policy will be issued.

At closing, all agents, buyers, and sellers meet to sign the closing documents and exchange money, keys, and warranties (if any). The closing agent will overnight or courier the deed, mortgages, and more to the courthouse for recording.

It's really basic. All you need to do is make sure that you have everything in writing from the bank and the new buyer for your closing to go smoothly. The closing agent will handle everything for you. It will be an easy, stress-free day.

Check Your Credit after the Deal Is Done

We feel that it is very important to check your credit once the closing is complete. If you worked out a deed in lieu or a short sale and the bank agreed to satisfy the loan as "payment in full," you want to make sure your credit report reflects that. You should have it in writing so that if the bank places something on your credit report that was not agreed upon, you have proof and can force the bank and credit bureau to correct it.

If the bank agreed to full satisfaction, then that needs to be reflected on your credit report. Sometimes banks will put "satisfied with a short sale" or "satisfied with a deed in lieu of foreclosure" on your credit. Although these are better than "foreclosure," a simple "satisfaction" is best. A satisfaction shows future creditors that you were able to solve the problem.

When you want to buy a new car, the salesperson pulls your credit report and looks at your history. He is most interested in how timely you paid your last car payment. Likewise, when you want to buy a new house, the mortgage company wants to see how timely you paid your last mortgage payment. The companies are less concerned with how you pay other bills. They want to see that you are concerned with paying your car or house on time. You can have late mortgage payments and still get a car loan as long as the prior car payments were paid on time.

The great news is that your credit will not be ruined forever. It will take time to reestablish it though. You'll have to wait 30 to 60 days to check your credit. The bank has to report it to the credit bureau and they need time to file it. Your credit should reflect the changes by the next credit cycle.

Ordering Your Free Annual Credit Report

The three nationwide consumer reporting companies have set up one central web site, toll-free telephone number, and mailing address through which you can order your free annual report. To order, click on annualcreditreport.com, call (877) 322-8228, or complete the Annual Credit Report Request Form and mail it to:

Annual Credit Report Request Service
P.O. Box 105281
Atlanta, GA 30348-5281

Do not contact the three nationwide consumer reporting companies individually. They only provide free annual credit reports through the above contact.

PART III

Other Options and Issues for Underwater Homeowners

CHAPTER 11

If Nothing Else Works, Consider Bankruptcy

O kay—you have tried every-thing:

➤ Selling the property yourself.

➤ Selling the property using a real estate agent.

➤ A forbearance agreement.

➤ A loan modification.

➤ Tried to do your own short sale.

➤ Had an investor try a short sale for you.

Nothing has worked. Your depression is starting to come back, the stress is building again, it seems hopeless, it is looking like there is no help in sight—we have great news—there are still a few options left to try before losing your property to the bank.

In the next chapters, we are going to cover your final options. If none of these options work, then foreclosure may be imminent. Even with all your hard work, sometimes nothing can be done. Often you run into logistical problems:

➤ The bank has too many foreclosures to process.

➤ The bank ran up a large bill with the attorney and wants to cut losses.

➤ The bank may be overcommitted until the next quarter.

- ➤ The stocks are dropping for the bank.

- ➤ The bank has decided to take the property and sell it retail.

- ➤ Many times the banks just have too many foreclosures to process before the sheriff's sale.

- ➤ There are not enough loss mitigation representatives to process all the short sales.

- ➤ You live in a state where the foreclosure process is very short—Georgia, Texas, Virginia, and a few others. Check with your local Real Estate Investment Association (REIA) because foreclosure time frames can change.

- ➤ Your loss mitigation representative quit before you could get the deal approved.

- ➤ The bank sold the note to another bank that does not do short sales.

Sadly, the options that are left are not the easiest to deal with emotionally.

Deeding the house back to the bank can hurt your credit, living with negative cash flow may not be possible, and renting your house out to someone else can be humiliating.

We started with what we consider to be the best options first—selling the house, doing a forbearance agreement, a loan modification, or a short sale. These options give you a cleaner break or a fresher start. The options that are left leave you no choice but to go in the hole financially each month, deal with a tenant, or lose the house in foreclosure.

Remember what we keep saying—*it is okay to walk away*. There is no shame in leaving a house behind, renting for a while, and then starting over when the time is right. As we told you earlier, Henry Ford went bankrupt five times. He completely failed and closed companies, lost employees, was ridiculed by others, yet kept going. What gave him the determination to keep going? Something inside drove him to success. We have both had foreclosures, bankruptcies, divorces, and more. What drove us to succeed? We both wanted a good life for ourselves and our kids and were willing to work hard to make it happen. Every failure you have puts you one step closer to a success.

The key is to keep trying. Never give up, never let anyone tell you that you are not worth it, never sweat the small stuff. In the end, it is all small stuff.

While we were writing this book, we read about a woman who committed suicide over her pending foreclosure. The article said that her foreclosure sale was scheduled for 5:30 that day. At 2:30 she faxed a suicide note to the bank stating that she would be dead by the time the auction was held at 5:30. The bank sent the police to the house and they found the woman dead of a gunshot wound to the head. We were so sad to read that.

Folks—this is a piece of property, it is an object, it does not have feelings, *it does not love you back*, and it can be replaced. If you were told today that you had cancer, the house would be the least of your worries. Please don't lose another minute's sleep over this situation. You will recover and you will be better off than you were before. We are living proof.

Let's look at the final options you have left. Again, whether an investor or a homeowner, these options will work for you:

- ➤ Do a deed in lieu of foreclosure.
- ➤ Ride out the storm.
- ➤ Live with negative cash flow.
- ➤ Rent the house.
- ➤ Simply walk away and start over.

Bankruptcy—How to Buy Time

Usually when a homeowner in foreclosure or an investor losing properties contacts an attorney for advice, the attorney will advise them to file bankruptcy. A common misunderstanding is that by filing bankruptcy you don't owe the bank anything. We have sat with so many homeowners who told us they could just file bankruptcy and keep the house. If that were true, why wouldn't we all buy a $5 million house, file bankruptcy, and keep the house? Bankruptcy only stalls the foreclosure process.

Attorneys use bankruptcy as a tool to stall the sheriff's sale and buy their clients time.

There are three types of bankruptcies:

1. **Chapter 13:** Used for homeowners who want to restructure their payments.
2. **Chapter 7:** Used for homeowners who want to absolve their debt and walk away.
3. **Chapter 11:** Used for businesses and corporations.

Most of you would file a Chapter 7 or Chapter 13. There is a government web site www.uscourts.gov that will take care of all your bankruptcy questions. You can download free papers, read explanations, take credit counseling online, and much more—at no cost. The site makes it very easy for a homeowner to file bankruptcy and buy time with the court system.

All you have to do is download the papers for the bankruptcy you want to file, fill out the papers, take them to the courthouse, get a certified copy made, take it to the person selling your property, and stop the sale. It really is that easy. The court will order a 341 hearing, which is a hearing for your creditors, and work out a plan for you.

We *never* recommend that anyone file bankruptcy without employing an attorney. The benefit of filing bankruptcy is that it buys time and stalls the sheriff's sale indefinitely.

Here is how an attorney will explain it to you:

> Wait until a week before the sheriff's sale.
> File a Chapter 13 to stop the foreclosure sale.
> The court will set a 341 hearing—usually in 30 to 45 days from when you file.

You will go to court and ask the judge to work out a repayment plan.

You will do your best to make payments.

If you can't make these payments accordingly, the judge could kick you out of bankruptcy.

During this time, the bank can't sell your house without filing a "motion for relief from stay" with the court system and getting the judge to approve it.

When that happens, you "roll" your Chapter 13 into a Chapter 7.

With a Chapter 7, you will get another 341 hearing that buys another 30 to 45 days.

The judge will decide what you get to keep, what must be sold, and what must be paid back.

Once it is all said and done, the bankruptcy is discharged.

If a homeowner went from a Chapter 13 into a Chapter 7, this could take well over a year. During this year, the homeowner would not have to make mortgage payments. Many homeowners choose this option so that they can save money and prepare to move. The downside to this option is that the homeowner is constantly bombarded with collection calls, court hearings, being served papers, and more. It is extremely stressful to be in bankruptcy for this long. It is an option though. If you have tried everything and nothing has worked and you need time to save a few bucks to move with, you could file bankruptcy with an attorney's approval.

Whether you file a Chapter 7 or a Chapter 13, your credit will reflect that you filed bankruptcy. As long as you work things out before the final discharge of the bankruptcy, your credit will show that a bankruptcy was filed, but worked out.

When doing a short sale, whether by yourself or with the help of an investor, the threat of bankruptcy is usually enough to get the bank to listen. The bank knows that you could file bankruptcy and live free for a year or more. Remember, the bank does not want to *own* property, it wants to *lend* money.

Keep in mind that bankruptcy is not a solution; it is a stall tactic. It will buy you time to work out a solution. Unless you can get into a Chapter 13 and repay everything, you will eventually still lose your property. Personally, we think bankruptcy causes too much stress on top of a foreclosure. We'd rather see you work out a solution that gets you a fresh start as soon as possible.

Will Bankruptcy Help or Hurt My Credit?

As we mentioned earlier, bankruptcy often helps more than it hurts. Look at it from a creditors' point of view. If you have been making late payments on everything for two years and suddenly your payments start on time again, the creditors are going to watch you for a while to see if you continue to make on-time payments.

If you file bankruptcy, it is like wiping the slate clean. You start fresh. If you make all your payments on time for two years, you can buy another house, car, get credit cards, and whatever else you want.

We had a friend who went through a nasty divorce and filed bankruptcy. Her husband had run up thousands and thousands of dollars in credit card debt to get even with her for leaving him (he was abusive) and there was no way to pay the debts off. He didn't care about his credit and wanted to drag her down with him. She filed a Chapter 7. We gave her advice on how to repair her credit and two years later she had a credit score of over 700! It was awesome to watch her drive off the car lot with a brand new car and no down payment. Friends, you will have good credit again, you will be able to buy another house, invest in more properties, own a new car, and much more.

Unless you have a lot of credit card debt or a huge deficiency judgment, bankruptcy may not be the answer. If you are only behind on mortgage payments and have paid everything else on time, bankruptcy may hurt more than it will help.

This is a good time to go the government site—www.uscourts.gov and take a look at the Chapter 7 and Chapter 13 papers and see if one of those might be right for you. Only an attorney can advise you on what to do; we can only give our opinion—which is NOT legal advice.

Bottom line—bankruptcy can actually help if you are buried; it can hurt if you are not. If you do file, make sure to list everything, including your deficiency judgment. You don't want to file and not list everything and still owe money. If you are going to do it, it needs to be a clean break.

We found the following information on www.uscourts.gov to be helpful. Check out the site yourself for more information.

United States Bankruptcy Courts

Each of the 94 federal judicial districts handles bankruptcy matters, and in almost all districts, bankruptcy cases are filed in the federal courthouse. Bankruptcy cases cannot be filed in state or county court. Bankruptcy laws help people who can no longer pay their creditors get a fresh start by liquidating their assets to pay their debts, or by creating a repayment plan.

Bankruptcy laws also protect troubled businesses and provide for fair distributions to business creditors through reorganization or liquidation. These procedures are covered under Title 11 of the United States Code.

Filing for Bankruptcy

When you file bankruptcy your creditors, court personnel, the media, and general public are notified. An official notice will be placed in the legal section of your newspaper stating that you filed and giving other creditors a chance to join in. The court will set a 341 hearing and the process will begin.

In 2005, the Bankruptcy Code was amended to require that anyone filing bankruptcy complete an **approved** credit counseling program before they file bankruptcy. Most people can now do the class online. Again, go to the web site to find a list of approved agencies and complete the course before you file. It only takes a few hours.

Filing for Bankruptcy without an Attorney Corporations and partnerships must have an attorney to file a bankruptcy case. Individuals, however, may represent themselves in bankruptcy court. Individuals can file bankruptcy without an attorney; to represent yourself is called filing "pro se." To buy additional time, many homeowners will file bankruptcy themselves and hire an attorney afterward; the attorney will ask for a dismissal of the case and then refile, often buying 90 days or more before the individual must appear in court. Bankruptcy is not something to toy with. If you do file yourself, hire an attorney as soon as possible. **Bankruptcy has long-term financial and legal consequences—hiring a competent attorney is strongly recommended.**

Debtors must list all property and debts in their bankruptcy paperwork. If a debt is not listed, it is possible the debt will not be discharged. The judge can also deny the discharge of all debts if a debtor does something dishonest in connection with the bankruptcy case, such as destroying or hiding property, falsifying records, or lying. Individual bankruptcy cases are randomly audited to determine the accuracy, truthfulness, and completeness of the information that the debtor is required to provide. **Please be aware that bankruptcy fraud is a crime.**

Credit Counseling

Individual debtors are generally required to obtain credit counseling from an approved provider within 180 days before filing a case, and to file a statement of compliance and a certificate of credit counseling furnished by the provider. Failure to do so may result in dismissal of the case, however; in most cases, if you file bankruptcy without completing the credit counseling, the court will require completion of the counseling before your first hearing giving you time to stay within the guidelines.

Finding an Attorney, Including Free Legal Services

Debtors are strongly encouraged to obtain the services of competent legal counsel. Even if you cannot afford to pay an attorney, you may be able to qualify for free legal services. For information about hiring an attorney, or about free (also known as *pro bono*) legal services, contact your state or local bar association. Many law schools have legal clinics that offer free legal services. Court web sites often have contact information for bar associations and pro bono legal service programs, as well as important procedural information.

For information about such legal resources, check the American Bar Association's Legal Help page, the Legal Services Corporation, or the web site of the bankruptcy court where you intend to file.

If you are filing or involved in a bankruptcy case and do not have an attorney, the web site of the bankruptcy court where the case has been or will be filed may be of assistance. The Bankruptcy Resources page may be of help as well.

As you can see, filing bankruptcy is not difficult to do and may be your best option. Seek legal advice!

If you are an investor, never help a homeowner file bankruptcy by downloading the papers for them or driving them to the courthouse or lending them the money to file the paperwork, you could be held accountable as practicing law. You do not want the bar breathing down your neck.

CHAPTER 12

Temporarily Renting Your Home

Right about now, most of you are thinking, "I'd rather die than rent my house to someone else." We completely understand how you feel. However, this is a viable option. Maybe your mortgage payment is $1,500 a month and your house will rent for $1,500. You could rent a smaller apartment for one year, get back on your feet, and move back into the house. The reason we don't like this option is because we don't want our family and friends to know we are having a hard time. We'd rather sell or lose our house and make up a story to tell people rather than let them see us move into a smaller place. I mean—come on—how degrading. Sound familiar? Friends, this is called pride. We know how you feel. We were once where some of you are right now. We promise that there is life after foreclosure, there is life after hard times, there is life after divorce—and it will be a better life.

If renting is something you are going to consider, here are a few tips to help you pick the right tenant:

➤ First, and foremost—go to these sites and do a complete background check on anyone you are considering renting to:

   ➤ **www.tenantauthority.com?aff=1169/** This site will give you credit and past rental history.

   ➤ **www.trackandscreen.com?aff=1165/** This site will give you employment history.

➤ Run a credit check—people are entitled to one free credit check a year. Have the prospective tenants pull their credit and give you a copy.

➤ Get on the Internet and do a background check. If someone has a criminal background or judgments for nonpayment of rent, you want to know. A background check is a very important step, but one most people don't take the time to do. Remember, you may want to move back into this house at some point, so take this step.

➤ Call the landlord from the property they rented *before* this one. The current landlord might want to get rid of the tenant and will give a good reference just to get them out. The landlord before this one is more likely to tell you the truth.

➤ Let the tenant know that this is a one or two year lease and that you are planning to move back in. Make sure they are fine with moving again next year. Often tenants want to stay put for several years at a time.

➤ Ask if they might be interested in buying the property if you should decide to sell. Once you move out, you may find that you really don't want to move back in.

➤ Collect a security deposit that is larger than the monthly rent. Most people collect first month's rent, last month's rent, and a security deposit. If the security deposit is the same as the rent, most tenants will tell you to use their security deposit and will not pay the second to the last month's rent. If the security deposit is more than the rent, the tenant will typically pay the rent to get the larger deposit back.

➤ Collect a nonrefundable pet deposit—at least $300 if the tenant has a pet.

➤ If the tenants move in friends or family members, collect an extra $200 per person per month. Be sure you have covered this in your rental agreement.

➤ Do not allow the tenant to sublease the property. This means the tenant would sign a lease with you and then rent your property to someone else. This is a common practice with investors, but most investors want a five-year lease from you.

➤ **Our best tip**—show up where the tenants currently live *unannounced* and see what condition their current rental is in. Whatever it looks like now is exactly what your house will look like in two or three months. If the tenants won't let us in, we don't rent to them. No matter how great the interview is with the tenants—you must see the inside of their current residence.

You may owe too much in back payments to use this rental option. For example, you may owe $7,000 in back payments and will collect first, last, and security. First, last, and security may only total $3,000. You are $4,000 short and can't come up with the rest of it. In this case, you would not be able to rent. Besides that, you are supposed to put the security deposit in a separate account. It is not your money. It belongs to the tenant and the tenant gets it back if the property is in good condition when he or she leaves.

Renting can be a good option if you are not too far behind in payments. Take the rental process seriously. If you have no experience being a landlord, do what it takes to get a great tenant to make this a great experience. You may find that you like it and want to become a landlord in the future. Being a landlord is the best way to accumulate wealth in real estate.

Figure 12.1 shows the rental agreement we use. We know it is lengthy, but it is solid. Feel free to edit anything you want.

FIGURE 12.1   Sample Rental Agreement (Downloadable*)

(Check your area for validity)

THIS RENTAL AGREEMENT (the "Lease") is made this _____ day of _____, 20_____, by and between _____ ("Landlord") and _____ ("Tenant").

1.   Demise.   In consideration of and subject to all of the terms and conditions herein contained, Landlord leases to Tenant and Tenant leases from Landlord the following-described property: _____ (the "Property")

2.   Term.   The term of this Lease (the "term") shall commence on _____, 20___, and expire on _____, 20___. The fact that Tenant may occupy the Property prior to the Term shall in no way affect the Term.

3.   Move In Date.   The date that Tenant may take possession of the Property (the "Move in Date") shall be _____, 20___. If Landlord cannot give Tenant possession on the Move in Date because of construction or the holding over of a prior tenant or for any other reason, Landlord shall not be liable to Tenant in any respect for such delay. If the Move in Date is delayed for more than 15 days, Tenant may elect to terminate this Lease, provided however, that notice of such termination be either hand delivered or mailed through Certified or Registered Mail, Return Receipt Requested, and received by Landlord not later than the fifth day after Landlord has given Tenant notification of such delay. If Tenant elects to terminate this Lease, Landlord shall promptly return Tenant's security deposit.

4.   Rent.   (a)   Tenant agrees to pay rent ("rent") to Landlord in the following amounts per month for the Term: $_____ per month.

Rent reserved hereunder shall be payable in advance, without offset, deduction, or demand, on or before the first day of each month during the Term; provided, however, that if the Move in Date is on a date other than the first day of the month, on the Move In Date, Tenant shall pay to Landlord a prorated amount upon the remaining days in the month. Rent

FIGURE 12.1   (Continued)

shall be payable to "_____"at _____, or such other accounts or place as Landlord may at any time or from time to time give notice to Tenant.

(b)   If a rental payment is not paid by the fifth day after the date the Rent payment is due, then Tenant shall pay to Landlord a late charge of $_____ due on the sixth day after the date the Rent payment is due and will accrue daily at the rate of $_____ per day for each day thereafter so long as the full rental amount and late charge remains unpaid. Any payment made by Tenant shall be first applied to late charges, fines, service charges, maintenance charges, security deposits, and pet-related deposits and fees, past due Rent, and last to current Rent.

(c)   Tenant agrees to reimburse Landlord promptly in the amount of the loss, property damage, or cost of repairs or service (including plumbing) to the Property or any part thereof caused by negligence or improper use by Tenant, Tenant's agents, employees, independent contractors, invitees, family, or guests. Tenant shall be responsible for any damage resulting from windows or doors left open. Such reimbursement shall be due immediately upon demand by Landlord.

(d)   In addition to the Rent, any other payments which, by the terms of this Lease, Tenant is obligated to make to Landlord, including but not limited to utility charges, fines, and damage charges shall be deemed Rent.

(e)   If Tenant makes any payment by check and the check is returned for any reason, Tenant shall pay to Landlord a service charge of $50 in addition to any late charge that may apply.

(f)   The acceptance of payments by personal check shall not be deemed a waiver of Landlord's right to require that payments be made by good funds and if, during the Term, Tenant gives Landlord two checks which are returned and not paid, then all further payments due under this Lease shall be made by cashier's check or money order.

(g)   TENANT IS REMINDED THAT IF PAYMENT IS MADE BY A WORTHLESS CHECK, LANDLORD WILL PURSUE STATUES FROM THE STATE OF _____, WHICH IN SOME CASES PROVIDES FOR THE PAYMENT OF TRIPLE THE AMOUNT OWED.

(continued)

FIGURE 12.1 (*Continued*)

(h)   Landlord's failure or delay in demanding charges, or other sums due from Tenant, shall not be deemed a waiver thereof.

5.   Security Deposit.   Upon signing this Lease, Tenant has deposited with Landlord the total sum of $_____ as a Security Deposit to be held by Landlord until the Lease Agreement expires. At such time, provided all rents and additional charges are current and Tenant has caused no damage to the Property. Landlord will return Tenant's Security Deposit in accordance to the terms of this Lease Agreement.

6.   Use and Occupancy of the Property.   The Property shall be used by Tenant only as a private residence. A _____ bedroom house may be occupied by a maximum of _____ people at any given time. Landlord reserves the right to change this policy at any time without prior notice. All adult occupants of the Property and guarantors of the Lease must sign the Lease. Any adult occupant who fails to sign the Lease will be deemed a trespasser, will have no right of occupancy in the Property, and is subject to immediate removal from the Property by Landlord without judicial process. Tenant shall notify Landlord in writing of the name of any new occupant of the Property other than listed below. If approved, new occupants will pay $200 per person in additional rent. The Property will be occupied only by:

_____

_____

7.   Utilities.   Landlord will not furnish any utilities whatsoever to the Property. It is the Tenant's responsibility, at Tenant's expense, to supply utilities to the Property. Tenant agrees to pay all utility deposits required in connection with use of such utility.

Landlord may modify the method in which utilities are furnished to the Property and/or billed to Tenant during the Term. In the event Landlord chooses to so modify utility service to the Property, Landlord shall give Tenant at least 30 days' prior written notice of such modification and the amount by which Landlord charges shall be adjusted in respect of such modification and added to the Rent due hereunder.

FIGURE 12.1   *(Continued)*

Regarding electricity, Tenant shall supply Tenant's own light bulbs and lighting fixtures.

8.   Pet Policy.   Pets are/are not allowed. If allowed, a minimum of ___ dogs and ___ cats being indoor/outdoor pets only. A separate **non-refundable** Pet Security Deposit of $_____ per pet will be paid by Tenant to Landlord. Landlord has the right to interview all pets.

9.   Acceptance and Care of the Property.   Tenant has examined and accepted the Property subject to those items listed on the attached Move-In Inspection Report or, if the Property is not yet available for occupancy, with the Move-In Inspection Report signed by Tenant on or before the Move-In Date. Landlord, with reasonable diligence, will correct those defects so identified for correction on the Move-In Inspection Report. Defects and damages not identified on the report shall be deemed to have occurred during the Tenant's occupancy of the Property. Tenant shall take good care of the Property and shall at all times:

(a)   Comply with all obligations imposed upon Tenant as a tenant by applicable provisions of building, housing, and health codes;

(b)   Keep the Property clean and sanitary;

(c)   Not cause or allow any other person entering the Property by reason of the Tenant's occupancy to cause the Property or any part thereof to be unclean or unsanitary;

(d)   Promptly remove from the Property all garbage, trash, and waste in a clean and sanitary manner and deposit same in garbage dumpster(s) or receptacle(s) which may be provided by Landlord, but in most instances, Tenant must furnish.

(e)   Use and operate in a nondestructive manner all electrical, plumbing, sanitary, heating, ventilating, air-conditioning, and other facilities and appliances provided by Landlord;

(f)   Not destroy, deface, damage, impair, or remove any part of the Property nor permit any other person to do so;

(g)   Conduct himself or herself, and require other persons in the Property with his or her consent or by virtue of his living there, to conduct themselves in a manner that does not disturb the Tenant's neighbors or constitute a breach of the peace;

(continued)

FIGURE 12.1   (*Continued*)

(h)   Keep the front and back lawn of the Property mowed at a minimum of twice each month and keep all shrubbery in a manicured condition; and

(I)   Promptly pay damages for violations of any of the foregoing, such damages may be denominated as "fines" which the parties acknowledge are liquidated damages and not penalties and have been determined and may from time to time be determined because the exact amount of such damages are difficult to ascertain.

No alteration, addition or improvement may be made to the Property or any part thereof without prior written consent from Landlord. No holes shall be drilled into walls, ceilings, woodwork or floors. Tenant may not alter original locks, nor add additional locks without prior written consent from Landlord. Antenna installations (including citizens band radio antennas) are prohibited. No water beds or fish tanks are permitted without prior written consent from Landlord and Tenant must carry flotation bedding system insurance included in Tenant's renter's insurance policy in an amount deemed reasonable by Landlord to protect the Landlord against personal injury and damage to the Property. Any such policy shall name the Landlord as a loss payee. Tenant shall not remove Landlord's fixtures, appliances, furniture, or furnishings from the Property for any purpose.

Any permitted alterations, additions, and improvements made to the Property shall be at Tenant's sole cost and expense, shall be surrendered with the Property and shall become the property of Landlord at the expiration or sooner termination of the Lease.

If Tenant does not keep the lawn in the condition expressed in paragraph 9(h) above, Tenant will have a 10-day grace period after one written notice from Landlord, to put the lawn in the condition required by paragraph 9(h) above. If Tenant fails to do so, a \$_____ per month charge will be added to Tenant's Rent figure due hereunder beginning in the month the notice letter from Landlord was mailed, in order for Landlord to cover the expense of maintaining the lawn. The Rent will be deemed increased by \$_____ and said increased Rent will be the Rent now due hereunder.

FIGURE 12.1   *(Continued)*

10.   Holding Over.   For each day after the termination of the Lease that Tenant continues in possession of the Property without the permission of Landlord, Tenant shall pay to Landlord, in addition to all other damages provided for hereunder, the Security Deposit Agreement, and double the amount of Rent due on the Property based on a proration of the month Rent provided for herein.

11.   Rules and Regulations. Tenant and Tenant's family, guests, licensees, employees, agents and independent contractors shall comply with all rules and regulations now or hereafter promulgated by the Landlord, the community or any controlling homeowner's association.

12.   Landlord's Liability.   (a)   All personal property of Tenant, Tenant's family, guests, agents, employees, or servants located in the Property shall be and remain at Tenant's sole risk, and neither Landlord nor its manager, if any, nor either of their respective shareholders, officers, directors, or employees shall be liable for any damage to, or loss of such personal property arising from any of their acts of negligence or the acts of negligence of any other persons, nor from the leaking of the roof, nor from the leaking or overflowing of water or sewer, nor from heating or plumbing fixtures, nor from electric wires or fixtures, nor from any other cause whatsoever, nor shall the Landlord or its manager, if any, or their respective shareholders, officers, directors, or employees, be liable for any injury to the person of Tenant or any other persons in the Property; Tenant expressly agreeing to save Landlord harmless in all such cases.

(b)   If any of Landlord's or its manager's, if any, employees are requested to render any services to Tenant, including but not limited to, the moving of automobiles, handling of furniture, cleaning, signing for or delivering packages, such employee shall be deemed the agent of Tenant regardless of whether payment is arranged for such service; and Tenant agrees to indemnify and hold Landlord and its manager, if any, harmless from loss or damage to person or property suffered by any person caused by the rendering of such services.

(c)   Landlord shall in no event be liable for any damages caused by the involuntary interruption or failure of utility services whether furnished by Landlord or a utility company to the Property.

(continued)

FIGURE 12.1   (Continued)

(d)   Landlord shall in no event be liable for any damages caused by the interruption or failure, for any reason, of the cable TV and the security monitoring system, if any.

13.   Insurance.   Tenant shall do nothing and permit nothing to be done in the Property that will contravene any hazard insurance policy covering the same. If Tenant's use or occupancy of the Property increases the premium on any hazard insurance policy, Tenant shall pay such increase.

14.   Damage or Destruction of the Property.   (a)   Tenant shall immediately notify Landlord of any damage or destruction to the Property caused by fire, water, or other hazard. In addition, Tenant shall immediately notify Landlord of the malfunction of any appliances, equipment, or utilities furnished by Landlord.

(b)   If the damages are such that the Property is tenantable, Landlord shall make repairs with reasonable promptness and the Rent shall not abate.

(c)   If the Property is rendered uninhabitable due to the negligence of Tenant, its family, agents, guests, or employees, the Rent shall not abate.

(d)   If a portion of the Property is rendered uninhabitable by damage or destruction not caused by Tenant, a portion of the Rent shall be abated in a ratio equivalent to the ratio of the usable portion of the Property to the unusable portion of the Property.

(e)   If the entire Property is rendered uninhabitable by damage or destruction not caused by Tenant, its family, guests, agents, or employees, then unless Tenant is offered a substitute Property as hereafter provided, the Rent shall abate during the period that the Property is rendered uninhabitable.

(f)   If the Property is rendered uninhabitable, Landlord shall have the right to offer a comparable Property to Tenant for the remaining portion of the Term, in which event, all of Tenant's rights to the Property under this Lease shall terminate and Tenant shall be obligated to take and lease the substitute Property for the remainder of the Term and subject to all of the same terms and provisions of this Lease. This paragraph applies only if

FIGURE 12.1 *(Continued)*

Landlord has a vacant comparable Property at the same Rent price available and it is at Tenant's option to choose to accept the comparable property.

(g)   If the Property is rendered uninhabitable and Landlord does not offer a substitute Property to Tenant, Landlord shall have the option of either repairing the Property, in which case Tenant shall continue to be obligated under this Lease, or terminating this Lease, in which case Landlord's obligation to lease the Property and Tenant's obligation to pay Rent shall thereupon terminate.

(h)   The tenantability of the Property shall be determined by Landlord at its sole discretion.

15.   Right of Entry.   Landlord, its manager, if any, agents and employees, from time to time and at any reasonable time, shall have the right to enter the Property to inspect the Property, make repairs, decorations, alterations, or improvements, supply services, or exhibit to prospective or actual purchasers, mortgagees, workmen, or contractors without the consent of Tenant.

16.   Subletting and Assignment.   Subletting of the Property or assignment of the Lease is **prohibited** without the prior written consent of Landlord. Notwithstanding any permitted assignment or subletting, Tenant shall remain fully liable for the payment of the Rent and performance of all of Tenant's other obligations under the terms and provisions of this Lease. A consent to an assignment or sublet shall not be deemed a waiver of the requirement for consent for any subsequent assignments or sublets.

17.   Landlord's Obligations.   Landlord, at all times during the tenancy, shall comply with the requirements of applicable building, housing, and health codes, except for conditions created or caused by the negligent or wrongful act or omission of Tenant, a member of his family, or other person on the premises with his consent or as a result of his tenancy. Tenant hereby waives the obligation of Landlord pursuant to Florida Statutes, Section 83.52 (1987).

(continued)

FIGURE 12.1 *(Continued)*

18.   Default by Tenant.   (a)   If Tenant fails to pay Rent when due and the default continues for three (3) days (excluding Saturdays, Sundays, and legal holidays) after delivery of written demand by Landlord for payment of Rent or possession of the Property, Landlord may terminate this Lease.

(b)   If Tenant materially fails to comply with _____ (your state here) Statutes, Section _____ (statue number), or material provisions of this Lease, other than a failure to pay Rent, or reasonable rules or regulations, Landlord may:

(i)   If such noncompliance is of a nature that Tenant should not be given an opportunity to cure it or if the noncompliance constitutes a subsequent or continuing noncompliance within twelve (12) months of written warning by Landlord of a similar violation, deliver a written notice to Tenant specifying the noncompliance and of Landlord's intent to terminate this Lease by reason thereof. Examples of noncompliance which are of a nature that Tenant should not be given an opportunity to cure include, damage or misuse of Landlord's property by intentional act or a subsequent or continued unreasonable disturbance. In such event, Landlord may terminate this Lease, and Tenant shall have seven (7) days from the date that the notice is delivered to vacate the Property.

(ii)   If such noncompliance is of a nature that Tenant should be given an opportunity to cure it, deliver a written notice to Tenant specifying the noncompliance, including a notice that, if the noncompliance is not corrected within seven (7) days from the date that the written notice is delivered, Landlord shall terminate the Lease by reason thereof. Examples of such noncompliance which include, but are not limited to, having or permitting unauthorized pets, guests, vehicles, or parking, or failure to keep the Property clean and sanitary and so on.

(iii)   The delivery of written notice as required by subsections (I) and (II) shall be by mailing or delivery of a true copy thereof, or if Tenant is absent from the Property, by leaving a copy thereof at the Property.

FIGURE 12.1   *(Continued)*

(c)   In addition to the rights described herein, if Tenant fails to comply with the requirements of this Lease, Landlord may recover the damages caused by the noncompliance. Damages shall include, but are not limited to, all court costs and reasonable attorneys' fees incurred in connection therewith, collection agency fees, whether suit is brought or not, reasonable expenses necessary for the removal of personal property from the Property and for the reletting or attempted reletting of the Property, which shall include, but are not limited to, the cost of repairs and replacements, advertisements, commissions, brokerage fees, and other expenses caused by Tenant's breach of any of the terms and provisions of this Lease and the rent that would be due for the balance of the Term.

19.   Abandonment of the Property.   Should Tenant abandon the Property prior to the expiration of the Term, Tenant shall pay to Landlord damages for terminating the Lease in an amount equal to the sum of the following.

(i)   The amount of the Security Deposit.

(ii)   A short-term rent charge of $_____ per month for each month remaining on the Term.

(iii)   One month's Rent charge.

(iv)   A $_____ administrative fee for reletting the Property.

Landlord and Tenant agree that the foregoing are reasonable liquidated damages and not a penalty and that the exact calculation of damages would be difficult and not easily susceptible to proof.

ACTION WILL BE TAKEN TO SECURE A JUDGMENT AND COLLECT SUCH JUDGMENT SHOULD TENANT ABANDON THE PROPERTY WITHOUT PAYMENT OF ALL FINANCIAL OBLIGATIONS REQUIRED UNDER THIS LEASE. FAILURE TO MAKE THE PAYMENTS REQUIRED BY THIS LEASE MAY ADVERSELY AFFECT TENANT'S CREDIT RATING.

The liquidated damages provided by this section are solely to compensate Landlord for Tenant's abandonment of the Property before the expiration of the Term and are in addition to and not in lieu of any other damage that Landlord may have suffered by reason of any other breach by Tenant of any other provision of this Lease.

(continued)

FIGURE 12.1 *(Continued)*

20.   Landlord's Lien.   (a)   _____ (your state) Statutes, Section _____ (statue number) provides that Landlord has a lien on all personal property that Tenant located in the Property to secure the payment of accrued Rent due to Landlord under the lease. This lien is in addition to all other liens upon Tenant's property, which Landlord may acquire by law.

(b)   Tenant hereby gives and grants to Landlord a security interest to secure payment of all rentals and the other sums of money becoming due pursuant to this Lease from Tenant to Landlord and to secure the payment of any damage or loss which may be suffered by reason of the breach by Tenant of any covenant, agreement or condition contained herein upon all goods, wares, equipment, fixtures, furniture, improvements, and other personal property of Tenant presently or hereafter situated in the Property and all proceeds there from and such property shall not be removed there from without the consent of Landlord until all Rent and other payments due hereunder shall have first been paid and discharged and all of the other covenants, agreements, and conditions of this Lease have been fully complied with and performed by Tenant.

(c)   Landlord shall have all of the rights of a secured party as provided in _____ Statutes. Tenant acknowledges that notice of sale as reasonable has been given at least ten (10) days before the time of sale. Tenant agrees that a sale will be deemed to have been conducted in a commercially or residentially reasonable manner if made at the Property after the time, place, and method of sale and a general description of the types or property to be sold have been advertised in a daily newspaper published in the county in which the Property is located for five (5) consecutive days before the date of the sale. Tenant hereby gives and grants to Landlord an irrevocable power of attorney coupled with an interest to execute and file such financing statements as may be necessary to perfect the security interest of this Lease.

21.   Mortgages.   (a)   This Lease is and shall forever be subordinate and inferior to any and all mortgages now existing or hereafter given which encumber all or any part of the Property. Tenant shall not be

FIGURE 12.1 *(Continued)*

released from its obligations hereunder by a foreclosure of any such mortgage and Tenant shall attorn to any subsequent owner of the Property.

(b) Upon the transfer of title to the Property, Landlord shall be released and relieved of all obligations hereunder and Tenant shall look solely to the then owner of the Property for the performance of the duties of Landlord hereunder from and after the date of such transfer of title.

22. Tenant Information. Tenant has supplied information to Landlord by means of an Application or similar instrument. Tenant covenants that all such information was given voluntarily and knowingly by Tenant, and if such information proves to be false or misleading in any material respect, Tenant shall have committed a material default under this Lease that Tenant shall not be permitted to cure. Tenant has authorized Landlord to order and obtain a Consumer Report (Credit Report) from a Consumer Report Agency to be used in connection with the execution of this Lease. Tenant agrees to pay Landlord the cost of the report.

23. Successors. The terms and conditions of this Lease shall be binding upon and inure to the benefit of Landlord and Tenant and their respective heirs, executors, administrators, personal representatives, successors, and assigns (subject to Paragraph 17 thereof).

24. Notices. Any notice or document required or permitted to be delivered hereunder shall be deemed to be delivered, whether actually received or not, when deposited in the United States Mail, postage prepaid, addressed to Tenant at Tenant's address at the Property, and to Landlord at _____ (or at such other address or addresses as Landlord may at any time or from time to time designate to Tenant). Personal delivery of any such notice by Landlord or Tenant at the above addresses shall also be deemed effective delivery hereunder.

25. Rent Escalation. Anything to the contrary herein notwithstanding, in the event of increase in utilities, taxes, insurance premiums, maintenance costs, or other operating expenses of the Property, Landlord may increase the Rent by the amount of the increase

(continued)

FIGURE 12.1   (*Continued*)

upon thirty (30) days prior written notice to Tenant. The total Rent increase assessable by Landlord hereunder during the initial Term shall not exceed ten percent (10%) of the Rent set forth herein.

26.   Misc. Terms.   (a)   This Lease including any addendum now or hereafter added thereto is the entire agreement between the parties. No oral agreements have been entered into with respect to this Lease. This Lease shall not be modified except by an instrument in writing signed by Tenant and an officer of Landlord or its manger, if any.

(b)   IN THE EVENT OF MORE THAN ONE TENANT, EACH TENANT IS JOINTLY AND SEVERALLY LIABLE FOR EACH PROVISION OF THE LEASE.

(c)   Each Tenant states that he or she is of legal age to enter into a binding lease for lodging.

(d)   This Lease shall be governed by and construed in accordance with _____ law.

(e)   Time is of the essence of this Lease.

(f)   Manager, if any, is the agent of Landlord and may act as Landlord in all matters regarding this Lease until such time as Landlord has given a notice to Tenant notifying Tenant that such agency has been terminated. At such time and from time to time, Landlord may appoint a successor Manager to act as Landlord's agent with respect to this Lease. It is understood and agreed that all of the covenants, agreements, and obligations of Landlord hereunder are limited by and are made expressly subject to the terms and provisions of a written management agreement between Manager and Landlord.

27.   Severability.   If any clause or provision of this Lease is illegal, invalid, or unenforceable under present or future laws effective during the Term, then it is the intention of the parties hereto that the remainder of this Lease shall not be affected thereby.

28.   Attorneys' Fees.   In any action brought to enforce the provisions of this Lease or to recover damages arising out of a party's breach of any provision of this Lease, the prevailing party may recover reasonable court costs, including attorneys' fees, from the nonprevailing party.

FIGURE 12.1   *(Continued)*

29.   Security.   Tenant is aware that unlawful acts occur in the local community and that neither Landlord nor its manager, if any, can be held responsible for unlawful acts committed against Tenant's person or property or the person or property of any other person within the Property by reason of the Tenant's occupancy of the Property. The security of Tenant's and such other person's person and property is solely the responsibility of Tenant and neither Landlord nor its manager, if any, assume any responsibility in this regard.

30.   Waiver of Notice, Demand, or Claim.   Except as specifically provided in this Lease or by law, Tenant hereby waives the right to notice of any action, demand, or claim by Landlord.

READ THIS INSTRUMENT BEFORE SIGNING.

TENANT:

TENANT:

TENANT:

LANDLORD:

Print Name:

Tenants

Print Name:

Landlords

Witness:

(continued)

FIGURE 12.1   (*Continued*)

Witness:

_____

_____

_____

Print Name: _____   Print Name: _____

Date: _____, 20_____   Date: _____, 20_____

*Copyright © 2009 by Dwan-Bent Twyford and Bill Twyford. To download and customize this form for your personal use, please visit www.theieu.com/underwaterform.

Section 8 Program

If you have made the decision to rent your property or have vacant rentals right now, consider renting through our favorite government agency—Section 8 Housing.

We have several rentals in the Section 8 program—government subsidized housing—and we swear by it. Open the white pages of your phone book and find the local housing authority or go to www.hud.gov. Call and tell them that you have a property you would like to rent through the Section 8 program. Based on the beds and baths in your house, Section 8 will pay different amounts. For example—Section 8 pays more for a three-bedroom, two-bath property than it would a two-bedroom, one-bath property. Typically, Section 8 pays average rent for the county.

For example, we used to have rentals in Broward County, Florida (Fort Lauderdale). Then we bought a few rentals in Palm Beach County (West Palm Beach). We found out that Palm Beach County would pay as much as $300 a month more for the exact same house because the average rent in Palm Beach County was higher. Palm Beach County has Boca Raton, the island of Palm Beach, and places like that. These places caused a higher dollar per head in the Section 8 program. We sold what we had in Fort Lauderdale and bought everything in Palm Beach County. Check and see if the same is true in your area.

We realize that if you are renting your own house, you can't move it to another county, but you may find that you like the Section 8 program and may start buying rentals for your future. We are going to cover later how you can buy rentals right now, in your current situation, and build wealth.

Here are the facts about Section 8:

> ➤ All houses qualify for Section 8. As long as you are willing to accept what the government will pay for rent, your house qualifies.
>
> ➤ Section 8 tenants are not bad tenants. There is no such thing as a bad tenant to us . . . we screen heavily.
>
> ➤ The government pays the rent directly to you.
>
> ➤ You sign a lease for payment with the government. You have the right to sign an additional lease with the tenants—we recommend that you do this.
>
> ➤ Tenants cannot move out during the year. They get a voucher once a year and must stay put unless the condition of your property becomes unrentable.
>
> ➤ All properties must be inspected by a Section 8 inspector before they can be rented. Some states have an inspection twice a year. We love that because we always know the condition of our properties.
>
> ➤ The inspector is concerned about safety for the tenants so the inspector will make certain your property is safe.
>
> ➤ People in the Section 8 program live below the poverty level. The typical tenants are single moms with several children. They are not bad tenants—they are simply poor.
>
> ➤ The program is designed for the tenants to get an education while the government pays the bills. After their schooling is completed, the tenants are supposed to get a job and work their way off the program. It is not designed to be a lifelong program.
>
> ➤ Once tenants are working, the government will open a savings account for them and match what they save toward a down payment on their own home. Once enough money is saved, the tenants qualify for a loan through HUD, and then buy their own home.

It is a beautiful system when used properly. Most of our rentals are in the Section 8 program and we love it. The key to being a successful Section 8 landlord is to screen tenants. As we mentioned before, we show up unannounced and ask to see their current property. Keep in mind that most people in the Section 8 program will have several children. See how they live today to know what your property will look like tomorrow. Our children are well disciplined and help keep the house clean. We expect the same from others.

Since you are only going to rent your house for one or two years, Section 8 might be a perfect fit. Again, it won't work if you are thousands of dollars behind in your mortgage payment right now, but it will work if the trouble is just starting.

Each tenant in the Section 8 program has an assigned counselor. These counselors know the entire rental history of the tenants. The bad thing is that they are not allowed to give out derogatory information. We met with a counselor once for a heart-to-heart to determine what we can and can't ask. Although the counselors can't say the tenants trashed the last house, they can answer questions about the tenants' rental history.

Screening Section 8 Tenants: Questions to Ask the Counselor

> **How many times in the past two years have the tenants moved?** If the tenants have moved three times, it is safe to assume they were evicted. With the Section 8 program, tenants are placed on a one-year lease. If they move in the middle of the lease, of their own free will, they are not given a new voucher until the full year has expired. Assume your prospective tenants have a voucher for $800 per month. This means the government will pay $800 toward their rent. If you rent the property to them for $900, you will collect $100 directly from the tenant and $800 from the government. We believe it is best to take tenants whose voucher covers your entire amount. It is not worth having to drive all over town for $100 every month. The tenants are given one voucher a year. If their voucher is from January to December, they must move every

December 31 or sign a new lease. If the tenants break a lease and move in September, they will not receive government assistance again until January and they risk being kicked off the program. If you ask how many times they moved and it is more than once a year, they were most likely evicted by an unhappy landlord. While the tenants cannot break your lease, you can evict them for abusing your property.

➤ **What is the tenant's average rental term?** Do they move yearly, biyearly, or every five years. Tenants who are long-term renters are much better as they will likely stay at your place for years to come. We have several Section 8 tenants who have lived in our houses for seven and eight years. We love them because the government is paying down our mortgages!

➤ **Has another landlord ever filed a formal complaint against them?** In our area, if a landlord files a formal complaint, the tenants can be removed from the program permanently. Most tenants will not risk this.

➤ **Does the government pay for any damage the tenant does?** If you live in an area that does not reimburse landlords for their repair expenses, choose your tenants wisely. Our area does not, so we tell our tenants . . . if you destroy or do not take good care of our house, we will file a formal complaint and we WILL get you kicked off the program. As long as you take care of our place, we'll have a happy relationship. Our area will not pay for damage, but it will remove tenants who disrespect our houses. In most states, Section 8 opens its list only once a year and takes thousands of new names. We happened to stop in to the housing authority one day when the list was opened and people were lined up around the building since two in the morning just to get a chance to get on the list. More than 4,000 people showed up and there were 250 slots available. Many families wait years to get on the program. They are not about to blow it by destroying a house.

➤ **How large a security payment are you allowed to collect?** We ask for $1,200. It is amazing how many folks can come up with $1,200 when they live on government assistance. Where do they get the money? In our lease, we make them responsible for repairing everything. With a large deposit, the tenants are more likely to keep your place nice so they can get the deposit back at the end of the lease.

➤ **Can you use your own lease?** Most areas allow the landlords to use their own leases. Section 8 requires you to fill out government paperwork. Typically, you'll get a copy of the voucher, proof that the house is in good condition, has no lead-based paint, confirmation that the tenants have a voucher, and more. Typically, Section 8 does not want to get involved in the actual landlord/tenant lease. This is great for us because our lease makes our tenants responsible for everything.

Once you have determined that Section 8 is the way to go, simply place your property on the rental list and the tenants will call you. We typically have our properties rented in less than a week. There are more tenants than properties so they go quickly.

As with any tenant situation, your tenants are only as good as your screening process. For more information on Section 8 tenants and vouchers, see www.hud.gov.

CHAPTER 13

Don't Go Broke Trying to Save Your House

In this chapter, we are going to talk about staying put and riding out the storm. Unless you are very strong emotionally, have a **very** solid marriage, have a solid support system, and are prepared for months of emotional hardship, don't even consider this as an option.

We don't think you should consider this as an option anyway. It would stun you how many people use their life savings, all their retirement, borrow from family and friends, and *still* end up losing the house. Why would you put yourself through that? Just to save a piece of property? Trust us, your house does not love you back. It is not worth it.

We know that many of you think we sound cold and uncaring. We are trying to wake you up. The reality of the situation is that your house does not love you back; your rentals do not care if they sit empty; your furniture is not afraid of the dark so turn off the lights; your car does not care whether you made the car payment; your credit cards do not have to wear the latest fashion and don't care if your payments are on time or not; you get the idea? Your house does not care if the grass is mowed; it does not care if the roof is leaking or if it needs paint. You must let go of the emotional attachment. Once you are able to separate your emotions from the crazy life you are leading, the faster you will be able to move on.

When we first met, we didn't tell each other about our past hard times because we were worried what the other person would think. Once it came out, we laughed because we had been through similar problems during the same years. We both felt it made us better people. It took us years to be able to talk about our troubles in front of a class of students. We didn't want to be judged. We were worried that people would not respect us or want to learn from someone who had suffered financially in the past. As it turns out, sometimes the best teacher is the one who went through what you went through and can *truly* understand what you are feeling. We know that there is life after financial hardship—we want to make sure you know it, too.

Don't Go Broke

Do not use your life savings to keep your property. If you have not been able to sell the property or can't get the bank to do a loan modification or a forbearance or something along those lines, seriously consider giving the house back to the bank.

We recently bought a house from a couple in distress. As they began to tell us their story, our hearts broke. This couple was in their 50s, had a severely handicapped son, used 100 percent of their savings, 100 percent of both retirements, borrowed from family and friends, and still lost the house. Now they are in their 50s with no retirement in sight, a foreclosure, and a bankruptcy on their credit report, and are starting over. At 50, we are supposed to think about winding down, not starting over like young couples in their 20s. They should have faced reality long before they did and walked away or called an investor sooner. It makes no sense to use all your retirement money to save a house. If you bought multiple properties to try and make it as an investor and are losing them, it's okay. You can start over again, just don't use every dime you have and all of your retirement savings to save what you have now. It is easier to start over and buy a new property knowing you can still retire.

While facing foreclosure, repeat the following affirmations to yourself to help you get through the day:

➤ My house does not love me.
➤ It is a piece of property and can be replaced.
➤ I deserve a fresh start in life.
➤ This will not ruin my life.
➤ I am a good person who got caught in a bad situation.

Say these things over and over again and your mind will soon begin to believe what you speak out loud. We know it sounds silly, but it does work.

Whenever we rehab a property, we say the same thing over and over to ourselves—we will not over-remodel, we will not over-remodel, we will not over-remodel. This keeps us from spending too much money on the rehab process. When we sell a property retail we say—we are not going to live here, we are not going to live here, we are not going to live here. This keeps us from getting emotionally attached to the outcome—the sales price.

We have positive affirmations written on our goal board that we read every day. Here are some of them:

➤ We have God's favor today.
➤ Today doors will open for us.
➤ Our students will be successful.
➤ We are blessed.
➤ Our family is blessed.
➤ Nothing that happens today will steal our joy, and other things like that.

Saying positive affirmations out loud does make a difference in your daily lives. Your mind will begin to believe what you speak out loud as truth. If you state negative comments all day—I am so stressed, my life is over, why do I make such stupid mistakes—your mind will begin to believe these things to be true. You are better than that and you deserve better.

Living with Negative Cash Flow

This is certainly an option, but difficult to do. For many of you, it may not be possible. If the negative cash flow is too great, you may have no choice but to use one of the many options we discussed earlier, even if it means just walking away. The only real way to live with negative cash flow is to increase your monthly income or cut back your expenses. We realize that you are painfully aware of this, but you may not know how to make changes or where to start.

Let's cover some things that you can do to cut back a little:

➤ Lower your electric bill—keep the air conditioning higher or the heat lower. Wear a sweater or a tank top depending on the season. You may be able to cut the bill $200 or more a month, which could help dramatically.

➤ Start clipping coupons for groceries, toiletries, cleaning supplies, personal care items, and so on. Some grocery stores even offer double coupon days on certain days of the week. The store is trying to bring in business on typically slow days. Many double coupon days are on Tuesday. That means if you have a coupon for $1.00 off, it would be worth $2.00 off on that day. This could cut your grocery bill in half. A family of four could cut their grocery bill by $300 a month or more by using coupons and shopping on a different day of the week.

➤ You may have to do without expensive meats like steak and use hamburger for a while. Hamburger Helper, Tuna Helper, and products of this sort help to stretch a dollar. But read the labels, it may be less expensive to buy what is in these "helpers" and save even more money.

➤ Cut your own grass.

➤ Clean your own swimming pool.

➤ Stop going to Starbucks every day for a $5.00 coffee.

➤ Stop smoking cigarettes and drinking beer. Cigarettes and beer are very costly.

➤ Quit going to convenience stores.

➤ Change your cell phone services and cut back on extra minutes and extra phones.

➤ Have a garage sale and get rid of **everything** you don't use. Don't keep items that "you might use again" someday. We never use those items . . . ever.

➤ Take the bus to work or car pool.

➤ Bicycle to work. It is great exercise and will help your mental state. We do it all the time.

➤ Stop driving the kids everywhere. Let them use public transportation or get rides from their friends or let them bicycle. When we were kids we rode our bikes everywhere, remember? We would ride for hours and not think twice about it.

➤ Stop being the errand runner for everyone.

➤ Don't shop for at least six months for anything except food and necessities.

➤ Let the kids use last years' backpacks.

➤ Buy clothes from a consignment store. Many of the clothes have never been worn and are in perfect condition. Many items still have the original tags on them.

➤ Put your kids on an allowance and make them buy anything that they want with their own money. We recommend giving your kids one dollar for each year of age. We gave our kids $12 a week when they were 12, $15 a week when they were 15 and so on. Allowance stopped the day they graduated high school. This way if you have more than one child, they all get paid based on age, which is fair to everyone. If our kids wanted something that cost $75, they had to save. We bought school clothes once a year and they had to buy everything else they wanted with their own money—movies with friends, skating, CDs, video games . . . everything. It teaches kids how to manage money and it saves you thousands of dollars a year.

There is no shame in cutting back. By cutting back on designer coffees, cigarettes, electricity, cell phones, and clipping coupons you could lower expenses by $500 a month or more. That might be just enough to keep your property until the market changes. Get the family involved and work together as a team.

Many parents try to hide hardship from their children and spouses. Telling the children is the best thing you could do. Getting them involved takes away the feelings of helplessness. Kids know when there is trouble brewing. Your family can pull together and make a chart of what can be sacrificed or cut back. Make this a team effort. It will stun you how resilient children can be.

Let's look at ways to increase income:

- ➤ If you have children, have them take on part-time jobs and contribute to the household expenses. They can babysit, get a paper route, help an elderly person, clean a neighbor's house, shovel snow, mow yards, walk dogs for neighbors, and so on. They might find it degrading at first, but they must understand that they are participating in the family's success. It will empower them.

- ➤ You or your spouse could both get part-time jobs. Maybe you could wait tables, work at a convenience store, work as a telemarketer at nights, or something along those lines. If you choose this option, work different days so that the children aren't alone.

- ➤ You could clean house for someone else.

- ➤ Take in laundry and do ironing for people.

- ➤ Cut the grass for the neighbors.

- ➤ Sell items laying around your house at the flea market on the weekends.

- ➤ If you have a basement, clean it up and rent it out. Lock the door to the main section of the house and make an entrance downstairs.

- ➤ Rent out extra rooms in your house.

- ➤ Rent your garage. You'd be surprised how many people need a place to store items or work on cars as a hobby.

➤ Turn your garage into a bedroom and rent it as an efficiency apartment.

➤ Get involved in a Multi-Level Marketing company. You won't make money today, but it can build a nice business over several months and will help you in the future. We are involved in one and make a ton of extra money every year.

➤ And the one no one wants to hear—get a cheaper car. No matter what you drive, try to sell it and get a less expensive car.

Be willing to do whatever it takes to make it happen. You might be pleasantly surprised just how much you can cut back or earn extra when you really put your mind to it. Pride is what keeps us from making the necessary cutbacks.

We know a woman who was behind on mortgage payments, but was unwilling to say no to her children. She bought her daughter a Coach purse for $200 while behind on payments. Her kids had to go to the best school, wear designer clothes, attend every dance, go to every birthday party with an expensive gift, and so much more.

Pride gets in the way most of the time. Again, there is no shame in cutting back. Cutting back and saving your house makes a great story to share with others and teaches your children a great lesson about teamwork.

If you own rentals and they are not cash flowing, it is going to be more difficult to stay afloat. Maybe you could sell one or two properties to pay down the others. Cutting coupons isn't going to help much if you have five empty rentals.

There are still many areas to cut back on:

➤ Get cheaper homeowners insurance.

➤ Call the mortgage company and ask for an interest rate reduction.

➤ Try a loan modification or forbearance agreement.

➤ Sell your residence and move into one of your rentals.

Living with the Emotional Stress

When trying to make tough decisions, we look at everything from three different angles. If you will look at your situation from each of these angles, it will be easier to make solid decisions during this time of hardship:

➢ Look at your current situation from your point of view.

➢ Look at it from the other person's point of view.

➢ Look at it from the outside looking in with no emotional attachment to either side.

When we have difficult decisions to make, we sit together, write each position on a pad of paper, and try to make as unemotional a decision as possible. Try this—it works. Here is how it might look if you put the facts about your pending foreclosure in writing:

➢ **Your point of view:** You are losing your house, behind on your payments, losing rentals, emotionally stressed, not sleeping at night, blaming others for your troubles, the banks are idiots, your boss is a loser for firing you, your spouse is a scumball for running off, God is mad at you, why do bad things happen to you, you never get a break, and the list goes on.

➢ **From the bank's point of view:** These people don't return calls, they are behind on payments and are costing us money, we have to go through the hassle of hiring an attorney to file foreclosure, why won't they just call us and work something out, why do we have to hunt people down to work out a plan, hope the homeowners don't file bankruptcy and drag this on, the markets are changing so fast, hope we don't get stuck with another foreclosure, and so on.

➢ **From a neutral third party:** Why are they trying to keep this house, why are they using all their retirement money just to live here, why are they so prideful, why won't they ask for help, why won't they just call the bank and work

something out, what's the big deal about moving and starting over, why do they insist in keeping up with the neighbors, why would anyone lose everything when they don't
have to, why did this person buy so many rentals with no
experience, and this list goes on, too.

By looking at all three angles, it makes the most sense to
move on. You don't need to live with the emotional stress of
a foreclosure. Simply accepting your situation and moving on
will change your life. Set yourself free ... let go.

CHAPTER 14

How to Rebuild Your Credit

By now you are getting bombarded with collection calls, companies who want to fix your credit, mortgage companies promising you a new loan, and so much more. It is time to take a breather. Rent for a while and just catch your breath. You have the rest of your life to buy another house, another car, get more credit cards, and so on. Enjoy the feeling of being free of the responsibility of a house for a while. Let all this sink in and make a new game plan.

Now is the time to start a goal board, to think about restoring your credit score, to move in the right direction, to learn what you did wrong last time and not do it again, to humble yourself to live in a smaller house, and do whatever soul searching you need to do. There is a Bible verse - Genesis 50:19 that says ... *what the enemy means for harm, God means for good ...* we live by that. We know that no matter what bad comes against us, God is already using it for something good.

We have both suffered financial problems in the past, we have suffered failed marriages, we have had hurtful things written about us on the Internet, we have had people accuse us of using religion to gain the trust of others ... sometimes it seems that the more public we become, the more negative stuff we read. Our friends tell us that we are "big enough" for people to talk about us now and that we should be excited. That is exactly how we look at it now.

In order to save what is left of your credit, sit down and take a realistic look at what you have to work with. Do you need to file bankruptcy? Do you need to use a credit repair service? Do you need to work out a repayment plan with your credit card companies? What do you realistically need to do to start fresh?

Credit Repair Services

There are so many companies that claim they can fix your credit. This is the company that we currently use when we help homeowners who have been in distress. This company charges $500 to do a complete credit repair. When we purchase a property from a homeowner, we pay for their credit repair. We know that someday they will want to buy a new house. Whether a homeowner or an investor, fixing your credit is a *must*. In most cases, this company can get foreclosures and bankruptcies off of your credit within one year. Some agencies charge upwards of $4,000 or more!

http://ieu.fixcreditbiz.com

Credit reporting agencies have 41 federal laws that must be followed in order to place an item on your credit report. These laws must be followed to the letter. If the credit reporting agency does not follow each of these laws ranging from how to place items on a credit report to how accurate their reporting is, they have to remove the item permanently. Credit repair companies **challenge** the bureaus and make them prove that they followed the law to the letter. Since 99 percent of the time the bureaus can't prove they followed the letter of the law—they must remove the item forever.

It is crazy for you to pay some extravagant fee for a service that you can get for less. The Fix Credit Biz web site lists some of the most frequently asked questions they get:

1. Who Are Fix Credit Biz? They are the nation's leading full service credit repair company producing expedited industry leading results. They successfully remove every form of negative credit, including bankruptcies, tax liens, judgments, foreclosures, repossessions, and much more.

2. What Makes Them the Nation's Leading Credit Repair Company? They are utilizing a 15-year-old process that is database driven utilizing the same technology as all the major Internet search engines and portal providers. This ensures high availability and quality of service for every client. They understand the necessity of delivering a first class service. Offering this is the reason for their extensive investment into proprietary software.

3. Is Credit Repair Legal? Yes, they leverage loopholes in the laws that govern the credit bureaus and creditors to permanently remove negative credit on behalf of clients. They are applying the knowledge gained over the past 15 years to force the credit bureaus and creditors to correct inaccuracies in their reporting. The permanent correction of these inaccuracies enables them to permanently remove every form of negative credit.

4. Can I Repair My Own Credit? Before we answer this question let us ask you a couple questions.

> ➤ Do you know how to read a copy of your credit report?
> ➤ Do you know the loopholes in the law to leverage for the permanent removal of a slow payment?
> ➤ Were you aware that there are numerous different strategies for credit repair and not all of them provide permanent removal?

Yes, you can attempt to repair your own credit. It is possible but not very probable.

5. How Does the Process Work? The process is very simple:

1. You submit your order online with payment.
2. The Fix Credit Biz people receive your order and pull credit on you.
3. They identify all the negative credit within your credit report.

4. They then create an account in an Outlook database (which e-mails your login information).

5. They then input every negative item for all three credit bureaus classifying each item and matching it with the appropriate loophole in the credit laws for removal.

6. Then they create a disputation that is sent directly to all three credit bureaus.

7. Next, you get a welcome packet that once again goes over the process and provides all of their support contact information.

8. You will receive reports in the mail from all three credit bureaus that will provide results. The only thing that you have to do to ensure maximum results is to fax or mail these reports and all correspondence from the three credit bureaus to the processing center and they do everything else.

9. You will receive reports/correspondence from all three credit bureaus every 45 days.

6. *Should I Pay My Collections?* It is very important that you understand how the paying of collections impacts your credit report. For this discussion, let's imagine you have a $65 medical collection. We know what you are thinking: Let me just pay them the $65 and get this taken care of. There are a couple of different scenarios when you pay a collection:

1. The collection agency collects your $65 and then just sells the debt to another collection agency.

2. The collection agency collects your $65 and then updates your credit report to a zero balance indicating that you no longer owe this debt. Now for the bad news—you just lowered your score. When the collection agency updated your credit report to a zero balance, it also updated the date of last activity. When a negative item is fresh, it carries a higher point value than after it seasons for a while. You just paid money to lower your credit score!

Fix Credit Biz is set up to permanently remove collections whether the debt has been paid or not.

7. *How Do I Handle Collection Agencies when They Call?* This is our favorite part—tell all collection agencies the following:

WE DO NOT HANDLE OUR BUSINESS OVER THE TELEPHONE.

PLEASE SEND US SOMETHING IN THE MAIL.

The collection agency obviously is not going to just hang up. Repeat this a couple of times to them and then just tell them the following: "I AM GOING TO HANG UP NOW" and simply hang up.

By law, they are *not* allowed to call you anymore and harass you. Collection companies can be fined thousands of dollars for continuing to call. Whether you register for a credit repair company or not, you can do this technique right now and sleep better at night.

8. *How Long Does the Process Take?* Every client receives results every 45 days. This 45-day cycle is called a "round of credit repair." Every client's credit repair needs are different because credit reports are like fingerprints; everyone's is different. In working with credit repair companies over the years, we see that most people fall into one of two categories:

Category 1: These are the clients who just need a small improvement of 50 points or less in their credit score to obtain the financing they are after.

Category 2: These are the clients who need more than a 50-point improvement in their credit score to obtain financing in the future.

In fact, most category 2 clients have two problems with their credit report. They obviously have negative credit in their credit report. This negative credit has restricted the client from getting further financing so the client has been forced to operate in a cash & carry mode. This cash & carry mode leaves the client without positive credit to pull the credit score up as the negative item are removed from the client's credit report. These clients will need to strengthen their credit with the addition of positive credit.

Most category 1 clients can start using their credit again after 2 to 3 rounds of credit repair. Category 2 clients need to allow 3 to 4 rounds before anticipating using their credit.

9. How Do I Strengthen My Credit through Adding Positive Credit? Positive credit can come in a couple different types. The strongest positive credit is open accounts that have never been paid late. Closed accounts that were paid off and never paid late are also positive credit; however, these credit lines do not carry the point value of open, never paid late credit lines. Fact—most low interest rate lender programs for home mortgages require a minimum of three open positive (never paid late) credit lines.

No credit repair company can guarantee results, but we have seen amazing things with the company that we use. We like it for two reasons—it is inexpensive and it is automated. Like we said, we have seen companies charge as much as $10,000 to repair your credit. Those companies do the exact same thing—they dispute credit reporting agencies by using the 41 Federal laws. Why pay so much?

If paying for a service is not in your budget right now, start saving for it. If you ended up with a foreclosure and/or a bankruptcy, you will need credit repair to start over sooner. Eventually, things will come off of your credit, but this is much faster and more detailed.

We want to add a disclaimer here: This is a credit repair company that we use. We don't own it, we don't work for it—we simply use it. It has been working great so far. With the crazy economy we are in, they could go out of business like many other companies have. Use caution before you pay anyone for any type of service.

Steps to Rebuilding Your Credit

If you decide that using a credit repair company is not in your budget, there are other ways to improve your credit score. Of course, it all starts with paying things on time. We find that there are two kinds of homeowners and investors:

➤ The homeowners or investors who paid everything on time, found themselves in a difficult time, and began to pay bills late for the first time in their lives.

➤ The homeowners or investors who pay everything late all the time and fell upon hard times because they mismanage money.

If you are a person who mismanages money, not only do you have to start life over again, you have to break your bad habits so you don't get into trouble again. If you fell behind because of hard times, getting back on track will be easier for you. The first step is to create new spending habits. It only takes 21 days to develop a new habit. If you do the same thing for 21 days, you reprogram your mind to accept it as normal. If you do it for another 21 days, you have set it in stone as a new way of life. Here are some steps to follow:

➤ Start by paying bills when they come in.

➤ Pay things early, when possible.

➤ Pick one day a week to grocery shop and don't buy anything in between trips. Don't forget about double coupon days.

➤ Stop going to the local convenience store for expensive coffee. Make it at home before you leave for work.

➤ Pack a lunch for work instead of eating out every day.

➤ Pack lunch for your kids. They don't need to eat at the cafeteria every day.

➤ Take a 15-minute walk at night. It will help you keep a clear mind.

➤ Take an evening adult class on money management.

- ➤ Read books on money management for 30 minutes at night before you fall asleep.

- ➤ Be aware of the fact that you must make changes in your life.

- ➤ Don't beat yourself up over your past mistakes. Move on immediately. Thinking of the past keeps you there.

- ➤ It is a new day and this is a new life. Make the best of it.

- ➤ Read positive affirmations out loud every day.

From this minute forward, when you want to buy something ask yourself this question: **Is this a want or a need?**

- ➤ A "want" might be a new pair of shoes; a "need" is a pair of shoes for work because you work on your feet all day and your old ones are worn out—not out of fashion.

- ➤ A want is new furniture; a need is buying used furniture because you are sitting on the floor.

- ➤ A want is a new car; a need is a used, sensible car that gets you from Point A to Point B.

- ➤ A want is to eat steak every night; a need is eating hamburger because it is affordable.

- ➤ A want is buying your kids a pair of $150 sneakers because everyone wears them; a need is buying shoes at Payless where you buy one and get one half price.

- ➤ A want is buying the latest fashions; a need is going to TJ Maxx and getting last years' fashions for 70 percent less and still looking good.

- ➤ A want is going on an expensive vacation; a need is going to the park for a picnic on a Saturday afternoon to clear your head.

Get the idea? Only buying what is a **true** need will change your financial habits forever. It is easy to convince yourself that something is a need when it is actually a want. Make this a lifelong rule.

Now that your spending is under control, let's get your credit score higher:

➤ Get a secured credit card immediately. Find a credit card company where you can pay a small deposit and are given a credit card equaling the amount of the deposit. Capital One offers a $500 dollar secured credit card.

➤ Use the card each month for gas or groceries and pay nearly all of it off every month.

➤ Only use **30 percent** of the credit limit. For example—if you have a $500 dollar card, only use $150 a month. By using only 30 percent of the limit, your credit score will rise faster. If you pay it off in full every month, the credit card company does not make any interest. By not making any interest, you are considered a credit deadbeat. By leaving a small amount on the card, it raises your credit score faster.

➤ Have your new landlord contact the credit bureaus to add your "on time" rent payments to your credit.

➤ Have a mortgage broker add your on-time electric, phone, and water payments to your credit report.

➤ Have your car insurance added to your credit report.

➤ Make sure your car payment is added to your credit report each month.

Anything that you are paying needs to be added to your credit report, if possible. The more on-time payments you make, the higher your credit score will go. Soon, you will have five months of on-time payments, then 12, then 24, and before you know it you will be able to buy a house again. Two years goes by really fast.

Take this time to reflect on your past (not dwell on it) and what you can do different in the future, learn who you are, and move ahead. There is a great life waiting for you—one that does not involve foreclosure or bankruptcy!

Formula for Paying Off Credit Cards

Bankruptcy laws changed in 2005 making it much harder to file bankruptcy and wipe out credit card debt. You now have to qualify for bankruptcy as well as attend credit counseling. You have to have at least $50,000 worth of debt to qualify for a Chapter 7 bankruptcy. The average American has $10,000 in credit card debt on any given day. If you pay the minimum payment, it will take you 30 years to pay off your debt. We want to share a simple, easy-to-follow formula for getting out of debt.

The biggest reason most folks find themselves in credit card debt is lack of self-control. We tend to buy on impulse. That is what the credit card companies count on ... *your taste for credit*. This formula will teach you self-control as well as help restore your credit.

Your first step is to call your credit card company. Explain to them that you are in financial trouble and want to cancel your accounts. They typically expect full payment in order to close the account; instead negotiate the interest rate down and have the account frozen. This way, your balance does not continue to grow.

Maybe the credit card company agrees to settle on 10 percent interest, opposed to the 29 percent interest you are probably paying, and the account is closed to new charges. Assuming you owe $10,000, you will save thousands by paying it off at 10 percent interest as opposed to 29 percent interest.

It looks like this:

Credit Card 1	Credit Card 2	Credit Card 3	Credit Card 4
You owe $1,000	Owe $2,000	Owe $3,000	Owe $4,000

To make this example easy to understand and follow, let's assume the minimum payment on each card is $100 after you negotiate the interest rates down. Start with the card with the smallest balance and double the minimum payment meaning you will pay $200 each month instead of $100. Continue to pay the minimum $100 on the three other cards. As soon as Card 1 is paid off, add that minimum payment of $200 to the $100 payment due on Card 2. Now you are paying Card 2 $300 per month. As soon as Card 2 is paid off, add the $300 per month to the $100 minimum balance due on Card 3. Now you are paying Card 3 $400 each month. As soon as Card 3 is paid off, move that $400 minimum payment to Card 4. In no time, all your cards will have a zero balance. It looks like Figure 14.1.

In just 22 months, you are out of debt! If you had paid the bare minimums without negotiating the interest rates, you would still have eight years of payments to go. If you filed bankruptcy, assuming you qualified, your credit would be ruined for seven years, unless you use a credit repair service. Following this easy formula, you are debt free in 22 months. During this 22-month period, your goal is develop self-discipline and not to get into trouble again.

FIGURE 14.1   Credit Card Payoff Plan

	Credit Card 1 $1,000 Owed	Credit Card 2 $2,000 Owed	Credit Card 3 $3,000 Owed	Credit Card 4 $4,000 Owed
Month 1	Pay $200	Pay $100	Pay $100	Pay $100
Month 2	Pay $200	Pay $100	Pay $100	Pay $100
Month 3	Pay $200	Pay $100	Pay $100	Pay $100
Month 4	Pay $200	Pay $100	Pay $100	Pay $100
Month 5	Pay $200	Pay $100	Pay $100	Pay $100
Month 6	1st Victory! →	**Pay $300**	Pay $100	Pay $100
Month 7		Pay $300	Pay $100	Pay $100
Month 8		Pay $300	Pay $100	Pay $100
Month 9		Pay $300	Pay $100	Pay $100
Month 10		Pay $300	Pay $100	Pay $100
Month 11		2nd Victory →	**Pay $400**	Pay $100
Month 12			Pay $400	Pay $100
Month 13			Pay $400	Pay $100
Month 14			Pay $400	Pay $100
Month 15			Pay $400	Pay $100
Month 16			3rd Victory →	**Pay $500**
Month 17				Pay $500
Month 18				Pay $500
Month 20				Pay $500
Month 21				Pay $500
Month 22		TOTAL VICTORY IN LESS THAN 2 YEARS!		

Having too much debt is simply a bad habit that you have to break. It takes 21 days to develop a habit and twice that to break it. Start new habits while getting out of debt. Take a new lease on life ... start working out, eat better, spend more time with your family, go to church, read the Bible, find things to do other than shop and spend money. We'll bet in 22 months, you'll be a new person! We were.

CHAPTER 15

Is There Life after Financial Disaster?

Well, it's all over. The house is gone, your rentals are gone, you have moved into a new place and settled in, and it is time to make a fresh start. You are wondering if there is a better life ahead of you. Is there? We say yes!

Most people are so burned out right now that they don't care if they ever own another property. It is normal to feel that way. However, let's look at it realistically. If you rent for the rest of your life, you are paying down someone else's mortgage and throwing your hard-earned money out the window. Now is a good time to start saving for another property. If you could put just 5 percent of your income into an emergency/new house/investing account, you'd be surprised how fast it adds up. It will take you two years to have good enough credit to buy another house. During these two years, make it a must to develop new money management skills.

You may already have great money management skills and your foreclosure was the result of something else. No matter, sharpen your skills, be prepared for the unknown, and get ready to tackle homeownership again.

Next time:

➤ Buy a house you can afford on one income if you are married.

➤ If you are single, your mortgage payment needs to be under 30 percent of your take-home income—remember we talked about this in the very beginning of the book.

➤ Do not buy another property unless all your credit cards are paid-off.

➤ Don't buy any rentals unless you can afford for them to sit empty for six months.

➤ Make sure you can save 10 percent of your income for emergencies.

➤ Most importantly—make sure your payment has a fixed rate and includes principal, interest, taxes, and insurance. No more creative loans!

How Do I Avoid Disaster Again?

The best way to avoid disaster again is to learn from your mistakes. We know that many of you suffered a hardship and could not help what happened to you. If you had been better prepared, you might have avoided disaster.

Every person reading this book should have:

➤ A life insurance policy.

➤ An insurance policy that pays off your mortgage in the event of death.

➤ Life insurance policies on your kids.

➤ A savings account.

➤ One credit card for emergencies only.

➤ Insurance on your car.

➤ Health insurance—if you think can't afford it, check with the government agencies. Medicaid is available for your children even if you can't afford it for yourself. Do not be too proud.

➤ Health insurance that pays your bills if you are ill or injured.

➤ A lower rent payment than your mortgage was so that you can save.

- A cheaper car that gets good gas mileage. If you can't sell your car because you own what it is worth, short sale it and buy a cheaper one.
- A job or two if needed for a while.
- Maybe a roommate to help with rent.

Do whatever it takes.

From Dwan

When my daughter Ayla was small, I was totally broke. I was in no way prepared to be a single mom. At that time, I could barely afford my bills let alone health insurance. I went to HUD, applied for Medicaid health insurance, and was approved. I felt like such a loser, like I had sunk to an all-time low. I was so horrified that I did not tell anyone. I cried all day. I always thought complete losers mooch off of the government and here I was in line with everyone else. I came to realize that government insurance is in place for a reason—we all need help from time to time. Recently, I was looking for something in my safe and I saw the Medicaid card. It brought back a wave of emotions, and I gave thanks to God for bringing me out of such a bad situation. I kept that card all these years to remind me of where I came from and what I was able to overcome. I never want to go back to those dark days. Those dark days are the reason I have such a heart for people and try to help whenever or however I can. This is the first time I have ever shared this with anyone. I had never even told Bill. I am not embarrassed anymore because I realize that I was in a season, it was a hard one, and I was willing to do whatever it took to get out of it. My daughter was more important than my pride. I swallowed a lot of pride in those days; in fact, I ate it for dinner every night.

Now, we have lots of insurance, retirement plans, long-term rentals, and more. We take time to plan ahead and we always consider—what if? Hard times can fall on anyone—rich and poor alike. Being prepared is your best asset.

Will I Be Able to Invest Again?

If you are an investor, it is possible to begin investing again right now. You'll need to find a good hard-money lender. Hard-money lenders are also known as equity lenders. They are investors who invest their money in mortgages based strictly on the equity in the property.

The reason for the term *hard-money* is that the interest rates are usually higher than those offered by conventional lenders. These loans almost always require several points just for the use of the money. A point is equal to 1 percent of the amount being borrowed. For example, if you borrow $50,000 and the hard-money lender or the mortgage broker brokering this loan requires 4 points, then you will pay $2,000 in points just to borrow the money. Also, these loans are generally interest only loans and are short-term. In other words, you might receive an interest rate of 15 percent with a one-year balloon. This means that the monthly mortgage payment you make will cover interest only and no portion of the payment, taxes, or insurance will decrease your principal balance.

Accordingly, regardless of the number of payments made, when you sell the property your outstanding loan balance will still be $50,000. A balloon mortgage simply means that at some date stated on the mortgage and note, the principal and accrued interest will balloon and become due in full on that date.

The main reason hard-money is so popular among investors is that it's available fast and **there's no qualifying.** When you make an offer on a property, time is of the essence. If you can close a transaction in 3 to 10 days with hard money rather than 30 to 45 days with contingent bank financing, you will get more offers accepted.

We began buying rentals using hard money. We would buy the property using a hard-money loan and then refinance the loan at the end of the year. Since you have suffered a foreclosure, you will need two years in order to get a decent conventional loan.

Let's look at an example: You find a property worth $100,000 and the homeowners owe $100,000 and are in distress. You follow this book and negotiate a short sale. The bank agrees to sell you the property for $50,000 dollars. Hard moneylenders will typically lend 65 percent of the property value. Meaning you could borrow up to $65,000 dollars. Let's say you borrow $50,000 and your loan has a 15 percent interest rate—a common hard-money interest rate. Your payment would be $625 a month.

$$\$50,000 \times 15 \text{ percent interest} = \$7,500$$

$$\frac{\$7,500}{12 \text{ payments}} = \$625$$

You'll also have to pay for one year's insurance in advance as well as property taxes. When you add the cost of the property insurance and taxes to the mortgage payment, if it cash flows, it could be a good deal.

Keep in mind that you just lost rentals to the foreclosure process. What are you going to do differently this time? We are big fans of the Section 8 program (see Chapter 7). We make sure that the amount paid by the government more than covers our expenses. We have had great luck with this program.

The best tip we can give you is to purchase properties that are in blue-collar neighborhoods, do not invest in pre-construction, and do not buy anything unless you can buy it for 50 percent of the value. We see investors every day who bought $300,000 properties that now rent for $1,200. That is a quick way to go broke. Buying houses with a mortgage payment of $625 should be a safe bet. Section 8 should pay that in any area. Check to be certain.

At the end of the two-year hard-money loan, your credit should be fine if you follow our advice. You would then contact a mortgage broker who would find a bank willing to refinance your properties. We never finance our properties over 60 percent of the value. Meaning, in two years you would refinance your properties with a conventional loan that includes principal, interest, taxes, and insurance and would borrow no more than $60,000. A $60,000 loan, including everything, should give you a payment between $500 and $600. If your property cash flowed at $625, it will still cash flow.

Many investors make the mistake of financing their properties to the max. They owe $95,000 on a $100,000 property. When the market changes and property values drop, they find themselves losing everything. Please don't make the same mistake twice.

Sharing Your Experience with Other Distressed Homeowners

Our country is full of support groups—people who share a common issue and come together to talk about it. Talking about it with someone who has been there, makes the problems seem smaller. Consider sharing your story with others. It will make you feel better and it makes the other homeowners feel better knowing that they are not alone.

We both know exactly how you feel. No matter how bad you think your situation is, there is always someone with a worse story. Whenever we meet anyone going through a difficult time, we listen and then share our story if it seems appropriate. Sometimes people just want to vent and not hear your story. They are too caught up in themselves right now. It's okay when that happens; we just lend a shoulder.

Maybe you could volunteer at a church or something along those lines to offer support and counseling for others. We offer financial counseling at our church for people in foreclosure. We live in such a small town and people call all the time. It is surprising at times. We listen, offer advice (if they want it), and let them know that they are not alone.

People going through a difficult time often feel isolated. They assume they are the only ones in the world who have gone through this particular problem. It is helpful to see others in the same dilemma, not that we should be happy that someone else is in trouble, but it is nice to know that we are not alone. Humans need love and acceptance all the time. We often feel unworthy of love when we are suffering. God will not give you more than you can handle, so have faith that you can and will handle this.

Share your story as often as you can to help heal you. When sharing, don't be negative and miserable about it; tell what good has come out of it. No one likes to be around someone negative. Negative people will suck the life right out of you. One negative person can bring down an entire room, while one positive person can't bring up the same room. Negativity spreads like cancer. Keep yours under control. The situation will be over soon, you can move on, take the lesson and learn from it, and share the positive with others. You'll be glad you did.

Consider Becoming a Real Estate Investor

Whether you worked out your own short sale, are a burned out investor, did a deed in lieu, or sold your house retail, you know more than most real estate investors and agents will ever know. Investors are notorious for picking up a piece of information here and there and trying to build a business around it. To be successful at anything, you need knowledge. We provide the knowledge that can make any investor successful. Whether experienced or not, we can help you become a millionaire, you can rebuild your life, you can make it to the top.

Through all of this you might realize how easy it is to get into financial trouble, how bad things can happen to good people, how much knowledge you actually have now, and want to share that knowledge with others. Many investors started off as homeowners in distress and turned this into a business.

You may be an investor who overleveraged yourself and lost everything. The good news is that you can start over. There is so much information in this book that will help you next time. Stay away from preconstruction, rentals, commercial properties, and focus on wholesaling for now.

There are many people in foreclosure who could use your help. By using the information in this book, you could make a difference in the lives of others. Consider coming to one of our live training classes. In fact, if you will e-mail our office with proof that you purchased this book, we will give you two free tickets to our next live training. We both personally teach for three full days. These tickets sell for $2,497 each. E-mail your receipt to www.dwan@theieu.com right now.

There are so many benefits of being an investor:

- ➤ You can work from home.
- ➤ You make your own hours.
- ➤ You get to help people who are confused and don't know what to do.
- ➤ You can make a lot of money doing short sales.
- ➤ You can send your kids to the best schools.
- ➤ You can help aging parents.
- ➤ You can retire early.
- ➤ You can retire wealthy.
- ➤ You can start a business that you can leave to your kids.

Before you consider becoming a real estate investor, make sure your heart is in it. There is nothing worse than a real estate investor who is in the business only for the money. If you do the right thing for people, the money will come. We have been greatly blessed by this business. The first question we ask ourselves in every deal is, "What is best for the homeowner?" We have done many deals and made no money whatsoever because there was not enough for us and the homeowner, too. We know we can always do another deal and that this is the homeowner's one chance to start over. We do what is best for them 100 percent of the time. The money naturally comes.

Make sure that you love what you do for a living. You give up one day of your life for it—is it worth it? You can't get this day back, so don't waste it. Whether good or bad, we love and appreciate every day of our lives. Every day is a gift from God. We hope this book has blessed you as much it as has us.

May God Bless and Reward You Always!